EMPLOYMENT
HEADACHES

A GUIDE FOR HR PROFESSIONALS

by

Harry Sherrard

**Grosvenor House
Publishing Limited**

This book is published by
Grosvenor House Publishing Ltd
28-30 High Street, Guildford, Surrey, GU1 3HY.
www.grosvenorhousepublishing.co.uk

A CIP record for this book
is available from the British Library

ISBN 978-1-908105-29-5

Publisher's note
Every possible effort has been made to ensure that the information contained
in this book is accurate at the time of going to press, and the publishers and
author cannot accept responsibility for any errors or omissions, however
caused. No responsibility for loss or damage occasioned to any person acting,
or refraining from action, as a result of the material in this publication can be
accepted by the editor, the publisher or the author.

Preface

Sherrards is a specialist employment law firm with a range of clients throughout the UK in the private, public and charitable sectors.

As well as advising our many clients on their employment law issues, we have become well known for our vibrant, educational and enjoyable workshops and presentations. About 500 delegates a year attend our events.

"Employment Headaches" is a compilation of some of the best material that we have used in our training events over the last few years, all fully updated.

All of the "Employment Headaches" are based on true life case histories presented to us by our clients, which makes this book unique amongst employment law and HR publications. Rather than reciting the law and giving general observations about best practice, this book actually tells you what to *do* in the diverse range of situations that people managers may encounter.

I hope that you enjoy reading the book as much as we enjoyed writing it, and delivering our courses.

Harry Sherrard
March 2011

Acknowlegements

I would like to acknowledge the contributions that have been made to Employment Headaches by the lawyers, HR Consultants and support staff over the years:

Dan Soanes
Roger Greenhalgh
Charlotte Mepham
Kim Nicol
Victoria Bevis
Jo Prior
Viv Whatford
Sarah Hammant
Kate Evans
Charlotte Bruce
Sofie Lyeklint
Lorraine Sherrard
Celine Findlay

About The Author

Harry Sherrard is the principal of Sherrards, a leading provider of employment law, HR consultancy and training services, and has been a specialist employment lawyer for approaching 20 years. He is recognised as one of the leading employment lawyers in the South of England. The Chambers Directory, considered the most authoritative in the profession, describes him as "Incredibly well regarded" by clients and fellow lawyers, and "an outstanding employment lawyer who gives consistently good advice".

Harry and his team cover the full range of employment law work, including redundancy and restructuring, business transfers, performance management, disciplinary and grievance, discrimination and the full range of issues encountered by employers, large and small. The firm also handles employment tribunals throughout the UK.

Harry writes and lectures widely on employment law issues, and has conducted numerous employment law and HR related training programmes for clients. He has appeared on BBC television speaking about employment law, and has also spoken on BBC and local radio on employment law related issues.

He is married with 3 children and lives in rural Sussex.

The firm's website is **www.harrysherrard.com**

Employment Headaches

PARENTAL RIGHTS AND SEX DISCRIMINATION

Question

An employee has participated in sexual banter in the workplace over a period of several years, and has now raised a grievance about sexual harassment. Is she likely to be successful in this claim given that she was a willing participant?

Solution

Provided that an employee has brought her claim within the correct time limits and she can demonstrate that the behaviour she has been subjected to amounts to unwanted conduct related to sex which has the 'purpose or effect' of violating her dignity or creating an intimidating, hostile, degrading, humiliating or offensive environment for her, she is likely to succeed in her claim.

The fact that she has herself participated in sexual banter does not necessarily mean that it cannot be deemed to be 'unwanted'. This point has recently been confirmed by the Employment Appeal Tribunal in the case of Munchkins Restaurant Ltd and another v Karmazyn 2009.

In this case there was evidence that the women who had brought sex discrimination claims against their employer had engaged in and even initiated sexual banter; however the tribunal found that they had only initiated and or engaged in the banter by way of a "coping mechanism", and as a way to divert the banter away from their own sex lives, and consequently upheld a finding against the employer. The EAT even compared the situation of the women who had put up with harassment to battered wives who have put up with violence even though it is unwelcome, commenting that 'putting up with it does not make it welcome'.

Ultimately, each case will turn on its facts, and the extent to which the employee initiated and/or engaged in the banter will be an important consideration for the tribunal hearing the case. Employers can still argue by way of a defence to such a claim that the fact that an employee participated in the banter demonstrates that the conduct was not unwanted and/or did not create an offensive environment for them. Such an argument, however, is not necessarily going to be easy to run, or an argument that is going to succeed.

Where employees' participation in the banter may have an impact, however, is in relation to the compensation awarded for injury to feelings. Where a tribunal upholds a finding of harassment there are three bands within which compensation can be awarded for injury to feelings:

Band	Award
Top band: for the most serious cases, such as where there has been a lengthy campaign of harassment. Awards can exceed this only in the most exceptional cases.	£18,000 - £30,000
Middle band: for serious cases which do not merit an award in the highest band.	£6,000 - £18,000
Bottom band: for less serious cases, such as a one-off incident or an isolated event.	£600 - £6,000

The fact that the employee here has engaged in the banter for several years should mean that the award is more likely to fall within the lower or middle band, depending on the extent of her involvement, as this may demonstrate that the employee's feelings are not that badly injured.

In addition, it is possible that the tribunal could reduce any compensation awarded to this employee on account of her contributory negligence. The tribunal have the power to make such a reduction where they find that the Claimant's conduct is such that it can be said to have contributed to the damage suffered. However, such reductions are rare.

Question

An employee brought a sex discrimination claim against the Company which was settled. As part of that settlement she left. Two years later she has re-applied for a vacancy which we have advertised. She is qualified for the role.

Are there any dangers if we decline to interview her or progress the application?

Solution

There is a danger of a victimisation claim here. Previously it was the case that employees could not bring post-employment victimisation claims, but this changed when the European Court of Justice held that the Equal Treatment Directive provides protection to employees against sex discrimination perpetrated by a company after they had left its employment in Coote v Granada Hospitality. In that case, an employee brought a sex discrimination claim against her former employer on the ground that she had been dismissed because of her pregnancy. She was still seeking other work nine months' later, and alleged that her difficulty finding employment was due to her former employer's refusal to provide a reference. The Court allowed her claim, and stated that the rules against sex discrimination applied, even though the employment relationship had been terminated.

There have been various other cases exploring this area of employment law, and it is now clear that an employee can bring a claim for post-termination victimisation.

If you decline to process this employee's application on the basis that she brought a sex discrimination claim against you, this would amount to victimisation, and if she brought a claim, she would be highly likely to succeed. Bearing this in mind, her previous claim should not be considered at all as part of the assessment of her application and suitability for the job. If she has the requisite qualifications and skills for the job, you should progress her application and consider her for the position. If, however, a more able or better qualified candidate emerges, you can recruit that person, and a victimisation claim would not succeed, as the appointment was on merit.

Question

A male employee makes a flexible working application, saying that he needs to work at home on Fridays so that he can look after an elderly relative as he has no carer available that day. How does the employer handle this?

Solution

Since April 2007, rights to request flexible working have been extended to the carers of adults. But this employee is missing the point. The purpose of flexible working is to enable employees to work, not look after relatives. The employee here seems to be suggesting that he would remain at home "working" whilst at the same time looking after his relative. That is not an acceptable outcome for the company and it would be justified in refusing this suggestion. Strictly, the employer would not necessarily have to put forward one of the eight grounds on which a flexible working can refused, since this is in reality not a valid flexible working application in the first place. In the early stages of dialogue between employer and employee, this should be pointed out to the employee and perhaps the suggestion made that the employee might like to drop to part time hours, working Monday to Thursday, with a commensurate drop in salary, so that Fridays are completely clear for the care of the relative. This then can go forward as a flexible working application.

Question

An employee is currently on maternity leave. Is she entitled to receive profit share and bonus relating to the period of her maternity leave?

Solution

The position regarding bonuses during maternity leave is a little uncertain. Generally speaking a woman on maternity leave is in a special situation, which cannot be compared to that of a man or a woman at work since such leave involves the suspension of the contract of employment. This means that a profit share and bonus relating just to the period of maternity leave can usually be withheld.

However, if the profit share and bonus relates to any period of time when the woman was actively at work the position is different. In such a case an employer's refusal to award a bonus to a woman on maternity leave at the time the bonus is granted would be unlawful discrimination. An employer would be allowed to pro rate the bonus just taking into account periods when the woman was actually at work but would not be allowed to withhold the bonus altogether. In addition, the two-week period of compulsory maternity leave immediately following the birth of a child must be treated as time worked for the purpose of calculating bonuses and profit share.

The basic position therefore is that if a bonus constitutes pay for work done the employer cannot refuse to award the bonus to a woman merely on the ground that she is on maternity leave, but the bonus may be reduced pro rata to reflect any time spent on maternity leave.

The law relating to discretionary loyalty bonuses is much less straightforward. During maternity leave women are entitled to benefit from all the terms of employment except for remuneration. It could be argued that a truly discretionary bonus does not count as remuneration, which would mean that it should be paid to women on maternity leave. However, it could equally be argued that a bonus as a monetary payment is remuneration, which would mean that it could be withheld from women on maternity leave.

Therefore, the questions to ask oneself are:

Is the bonus / profit share retroactive pay for work done? If so, the bonus must be paid but can be reduced pro rata for time spent on maternity leave.

Is the bonus a truly discretionary bonus to reward loyalty? If so, it does not have to be paid if you can argue that it counts as remuneration.

Question

Janet's long-term partner Joanne is pregnant. When Joanne has her baby, Janet plans to adopt it – so that both she and Joanne can have shared parental responsibility. Janet has approached you asking for information about the Company's Adoption Leave Policy.

What should you do?

Solution

Adoption Leave – like maternity leave – entitles an employee to up to 12 months' leave.

For the purposes of the Paternity and Adoption Leave Regulations, an adopting parent is only eligible to receive adoption leave if:

a.   They are the child's adopter;

b.   They have been continuously employed for 26 weeks; and

c.   They have notified an adoption agency that they agree the child should be placed with them.

The fact that adoption leave is only available to those who are newly matched to children through an agency means that step fathers and mothers are not eligible for adoption leave.

However, Janet could opt to take paternity leave in those circumstances. She cannot opt to take adoption/maternity leave - even if she intends to be the main carer - as she is not the mother of the child.

If they both adopted a child, however, they could decide between them which one should take the full adoption leave and which one should take paternity leave. They could also take parental leave – although this would be unpaid.

Question

Two employees with young children have come up with a job share proposal, but I am not happy with it. Where do I stand?

Solution

Employees who satisfy the eligibility criteria and who have not made a flexible working request within the past 12 months have the right to make a request to work flexibly, which could include a job share proposal. However, employees simply have a right to **make a request** and not a right to be **granted a request.** You can refuse a flexible working request provided you rely on one of the eight business reasons for refusing the request.

These are as follows:

- The burden of additional costs.
- Detrimental effect on ability to meet customer demand.
- Inability to re-organise work among existing staff.
- Inability to recruit additional staff.
- Detrimental impact on quality.
- Detrimental impact on performance.
- Insufficiency of work during the periods the employee proposes to work.
- Planned structural changes.

If refusing the request, you must do so on the basis of one of the above business reasons and not on the basis of the employee's personal circumstances. In selecting the ground for refusal the test is a subjective one on the part of the employer, however any facts quoted in the explanation must be accurate. You should ensure that you are able to back up any facts should they subsequently be disputed. A decision based on incorrect facts to reject an application would provide an employee with grounds to make a complaint to an employment tribunal.

Perhaps more importantly, another issue that you need to be aware of is that, assuming that the employees making the request are female employees, refusing their request could amount to indirect discrimination, entitling female employees to bring an employment tribunal claim. This is because you would be applying a practice or criterion which has a detrimental effect on more women than men as it is accepted by the tribunals that a greater number of women than men have caring responsibilities and therefore need to work flexibly. You can defend such a claim if you can objectively justify your decision, however this can be difficult to do, and you will need to have very convincing reasons. Often a more pragmatic approach is to consider alternative flexible working arrangements that will meet both the business's needs and those of the employee, rather than refusing the request outright and trying to justify your decision.

Question

You are about to fail an employee on probation when you discover that she is pregnant. The reason for the failure was partly based on absence. Is it safe to go ahead and dismiss?

Solution

If the absence was due to pregnancy related illness, then there is a potential trap here. It is automatically unfair to dismiss an employee for a reason related to pregnancy, and there is no qualifying period of service required for bringing this type of unfair dismissal claim, so the fact that she is still on probation with presumably less than 12 months' service has no bearing.

In addition, there is likely to be a sex discrimination claim as pregnant women have protection from any detriment caused by a reason connected with their pregnancy. Dismissal would be a detriment.

If the absence was for pregnancy related illness, there really is no safe solution. The only answer for the employer is to argue that a failure for probation was on performance, and to disregard the pregnancy related absence entirely. If the employer can genuinely say (and persuade a tribunal) that the performance and non-pregnancy related absence was such that there would have been a termination in any event, there will not be a finding of automatic unfair dismissal on the basis of pregnancy.

Question

We have several part time supervisors, both male and female. All of our managers are full time. There is now a managerial vacancy. Can I advertise this role as full time, knowing that the supervisors would like to apply, and so therefore I would be excluding all of the part time supervisors?

Solution

It is well established that if a female with caring responsibilities is prevented, without justification, from working part time then this can amount to indirect sex discrimination. This is because the tribunals accept that refusal to allow part time working will adversely affect women more than men as women are more likely to need to work part time as they have the primary caring responsibilities (normally this is caring responsibilities in relation to children, although this can also apply in relation to caring responsibilities for adults).

Consequently, if any of the part time supervisors that would like to apply for the role are female and currently working part time because of caring responsibilities, you would be well advised to offer these employees the opportunity to apply for the managerial position as a job share, or consider other flexible working alternative solutions that will enable these employees to carry out the role, rather than simply excluding them from the process altogether.

In these circumstances it is only the supervisors who are female with caring responsibilities who may have the ability to bring an indirect sex discrimination claim. Any male supervisors or female employees without caring responsibilities will not have grounds to bring a sex discrimination claim (or any other claim) as a result of them being unable to apply for the position as it is a full time role.

It is worth mentioning however that even if the role is eventually offered to someone who is able to perform the role full time, that employee may be eligible to make a flexible working request. Currently, parents of children under the age of 17 (or 18 for parents with disabled children) or carers of certain adults have the right to make flexible working requests. Further the Government has recently announced plans to extend this right to parents of children under the age of 18 from April 2011 and eventually to all employees.

If an employee makes a flexible working request this could include a request to perform the position part time or as a job share arrangement. An employer can still refuse the request by relying on one of the eight specified business reasons, but in so refusing a request care must be taken to ensure that you do not indirectly discriminate against a female employee with children or directly discriminate against any other employee because of a protected characteristic.

Question

A male and female are the last 2 candidates in a recruitment exercise. The male is appointed, as he has the better experience. The female says that she had a career break to have children, so it is unlawful sex discrimination, as her relative lack of experience in comparison with the male is due to her maternity leave. Is she correct?

Solution

Probably not.

She may be able to establish a sexually discriminatory effect. But while that is a necessary condition for establishing unlawful sex discrimination, it is not a sufficient condition.

As the other candidate has been preferred not because of his sex, but because of his better experience, she will not, on the face of it, succeed in a claim of direct sex discrimination. If she could establish that she had been turned down <u>on the grounds that</u> she had taken maternity leave then that would be direct sex discrimination: there would not even be any need for a male comparator. But, on the facts as stated, that argument will not run.

So she would have to argue that there was indirect sex discrimination. That is, that the employer had applied to her a provision, criterion or practice which

(a)   he applies or would apply equally to a man but —

(b)   which puts or would put women at a particular disadvantage when compared with men,

(c)   which puts her at that disadvantage, and

(d)   which he cannot show to be a proportionate means of achieving a legitimate aim.

The "provision, criterion or practice" is "experience". There may be some room for argument about whether – in using it solely as the "tie-breaker" between two otherwise equal candidates – the employer has "applied" it as required by that provision. But that argument is not strong. Whether the condition in (a) was met would be subject to (probably statistical) proof, and it will be important to make any statistical comparisons among the right pools: men and women who (experience apart) would be qualified for the post concerned. But it will probably not be difficult to convince a tribunal that – because women take Maternity Leave and men do not – applying a length of experience "provision, criterion or practice" does put women at a particular disadvantage when compared with men. Clearly, the fact that this woman has been turned down for this job puts her at a disadvantage: so the condition in (b) would be met. The difficulty she would face would be in showing that the condition in (c) was not met.

Although the drafting quoted above appears to place the burden of "justifying" a sexually discriminatory effect on the employer – "which he cannot show to be a proportionate means of achieving a legitimate aim" – there is a strong argument that, where "experience" is concerned, the burden is actually on the applicant/employee to prove that reliance on it is not justified. This arises from rulings of the European Court of Justice in two equal pay cases: Danfoss in 1989 and Cadman in 2006. Although those were concerned with whether differences in pay could be justified by differing lengths of service the principles enunciated by the ECJ appear to be of wider applicability. In holding that differences in pay could be justified by differing lengths of service the ECJ said, in Danfoss (a Danish case)

> "As regards the criterion of seniority, it cannot be ruled out [...] that [...] it may result in less favourable treatment of female workers than for male workers, insofar as women have entered the labour market more recently than men or are subject to more frequent interruptions of their careers. However, since seniority goes hand in hand with experience which generally places a worker in a better position to carry out his duties, it is permissible for the employer to reward it without the need to establish the importance which it takes on for the performance of the specific duties to be entrusted to the worker."

Cadman was a UK case referred by the Court of Appeal with the question

-   Where the use by an employer of the criterion of length of service as a determinant of pay has a disparate impact as between relevant male and female employees, does Article 141 EC require the employer to provide special justification for recourse to that criterion?

to which the ECJ replied

> "Since, as a general rule, recourse to the criterion of length of service is appropriate to attain the legitimate objective of rewarding experience acquired which enables the worker to perform his duties better, the employer does not have to establish specifically that recourse to that criterion is appropriate to attain that objective as regards a particular job, unless the worker provides evidence capable of raising serious doubts in that regard."

European jurisprudence, which the UK is bound to follow, therefore makes clear (at least in the context of pay) that – even though it may be to women's detriment – "rewarding experience" is to be legally presumed to be a legitimate aim which presumption will only be rebutted if the worker provides evidence raising "serious doubts" that it can be relevant in the specific case. In that context it seems most unlikely that a UK tribunal would hold – without more – that in using experience as the tie-breaker in selecting between two otherwise equal candidates an employer was not using a proportionate means of achieving a legitimate aim.

On that basis, the female applicant here would need to show not only that women in general and she in particular were disadvantaged by the employer's approach. She would also have to provide evidence capable of raising serious doubts that experience could be at all relevant to the appointment. On the facts as we know them, she has not begun to do that.

Question

We have had a sexual harassment claim and our investigation suggests that the action complained of really did happen. Not only that, but we feel that the manager who investigated and dealt with the grievance handled the whole thing really badly. We are now facing an ET claim. How bad could this case be?

Solution

1. Compensation

If the employee succeeds in her harassment claim, as seems highly likely, the first point to be aware of is that, unlike unfair dismissal cases, there is no cap on compensation awards that can be made in discrimination cases.

The amount that will be awarded will depend on the facts, but generally the tribunal has within its powers the discretion to award compensation under the following headings in discrimination cases:

a. **Financial loss including loss of earnings:** This will cover financial losses, which predominately will consist of loss of earnings from the date of the discriminatory act to whatever date in the future the tribunal decides. There is no cap on the amount a tribunal can award under this heading.

In a recent case, St Andrew's Catholic School v Blundell 2010, where an employer was found to have victimised an employee over a 4 month period following her return to work after bringing an unsuccessful sex discrimination claim against the school, the employee was awarded 5 years' compensation for loss of earnings under this heading.

b. **Injury to feelings**: A tribunal can also award a Claimant a sum by way of compensation for injured feelings. A Court of Appeal case, Vento v Chief Constable of West Yorkshire (No 2) 2003, established guidelines for awards for injury to feelings by setting three bands of potential awards. These bands have since been increased in line with inflation following another Court of Appeal case and are now as follows:

One of the highest awards for injury to feelings was made in the case of Manning v Safetell and Medland 2008. In this case the employee received an award of £30,000 for injury to feelings where it was found that she had been subjected to a catalogue of blatant discriminatory acts over a two year period related to her pregnancy.

c.   **Personal injury**: In addition to an award for injury to feelings, a tribunal can also award a discrete award for personal injury. Usually, such awards are made in respect of psychiatric injury. In the case of X v Y and Z 2004, an employee received an award of £28,500 for injury to feelings where she suffered a significant depressive disorder and post-traumatic stress symptoms resulting in IBS.

d.   **Aggravated damages**: Aggravated damages can be awarded in addition to an award for injury to feelings in very serious cases where the employer has acted in a 'high-handed, malicious, insulting or oppressive manner' which has aggravated the Claimant's injury. An award for aggravated damages must be to compensate the Claimant for the injury suffered and not to punish the employer. Aggravated damages have in the past been awarded where the employer has:

Band	Award
Top band: for the most serious cases, such as where there has been a lengthy campaign of harassment. Awards can exceed this only in the most exceptional cases.	£18,000 - £30,000
Middle band: for serious cases which do not merit an award in the highest band.	£6,000 - £18,000
Bottom band: for less serious cases, such as a one-off incident or an isolated event.	£600 - £6,000

-   attempted to cover up or trivialise wrong doing
-   failed to investigate complaints or take them seriously
-   promoted or rewarded the perpetrators of discrimination
-   continually failed to correct a problem which has led to discrimination

The cases where the highest awards have been made for aggravated damages have usually involved some element of high-handed conduct by the employer in conducting tribunal proceedings.

Depending on how badly the employer in this example dealt with the employee's grievance, an award for aggravated damages could be awarded.

e.   **Punitive or exemplary damages**: Such an award can be made to punish an employer where the compensation in itself is insufficient punishment but such an award can only ever be ordered in very limited circumstances, and as a result cases where an award for punitive or exemplary damages is made are extremely rare.

2.   **Recommendations:**

In addition to compensation the tribunal also has the power to make recommendations for the employer to take specified steps within a certain timeframe. The Equality Act 2010 in particular introduced a new power for tribunals to make recommendations affecting the wider workforce and not just the employee bringing the discrimination claim. As such a tribunal may recommend that an employer:

Introduces an equal opportunities policy

Ensures its harassment policy is more effectively implemented

Sets up a review panel to deal with equal opportunities, harassment and grievances

Re-trains staff

3.   **Declarations**

Finally, a tribunal may also make a declaration – a statement that the employer has violated the employee's rights.

AGE AND RETIREMENT

Question

Joe was 65 last month and is still working. Joe told his employer by the coffee machine one morning a couple of months ago that he didn't want to retire yet. The employer was happy for him to stay on. Joe was not given the right to request working beyond 65, and there were no meetings.

Has the employer done anything wrong?

Solution

No. Contrary to common misunderstanding, the 6 month retirement process is only triggered if the employer is in fact thinking of retiring an employee. If the employer and employee agree informally that employment will continue beyond 65, there is no requirement to notify the employee of the right to work after 65 etc. The employer can retire Joe at any time by commencing the 6 month procedure.

Furthermore, there is no need for any agreement between employer and employee that employment will continue at all. As long as the contract is not terminated it continues.

Question

Ernie was 65 a couple of weeks ago and retired on his 65th birthday. Ernie made no secret of the fact that he was very much looking forward to his retirement and that he had been planning to retire on his 65th birthday for some time. The employer knew of this through informal discussions and did nothing in terms of meetings and giving the right to request working beyond 65.

Has the employer done anything wrong?

Solution

No. As seen in the case of Joe, who did not retire at the age of 65, the 6 month retirement process is only triggered if the employer is in fact thinking of retiring an employee who does not want to retire. Since Ernie has made it clear that his retirement at 65 has been planned by him and is entirely voluntary, strictly the employer is under no obligation to initiate the retirement procedure. However, the employer does run a certain amount of risk here. If Ernie has a last minute change of heart and decides that he would like to continue working after 65, he would be entitled to carry on working. He would not in any way be bound by his earlier commitment to retire on his 65th birthday. The employer would then be required to initiate the 6 month procedure or alternatively the shorter 2 week procedure which would incur a financial penalty.

Question

Peter is 67 and works as an office maintenance engineer. Peter has developed a back condition which makes it difficult for him to climb ladders or to sit down or walk for more than 20 minutes without taking a break. The MD wants to retire Peter.

Could there be any difficulties in doing this?

Solution

Until 30th September 2011, under the Equality Act 2010, retiring an employee at 65 or over constitutes neither age discrimination nor unfair dismissal, as long as certain procedures are followed. Rather, it is a fair dismissal on the grounds of retirement.

Provided the procedures are followed, this is true even where – as here – the retirement is clearly a sham and the real reason for the dismissal is something else altogether.

The procedure (in brief) is:

(a) Less than 12 months but at least 6 months before the intended date of retirement, the employer writes to the employee notifying him of the intended retirement date and tells him he has the right to request to continue working beyond that date;

(b) If the employee makes a request, a meeting is arranged to discuss the request;

(c) If the employer turns down the request, the employee is given the right to appeal;

(d) If the employee does appeal, a further meeting is arranged and the outcome is expressed to the employee within a reasonable time.

Therefore, provided you follow this procedure, you can "retire" Peter without risk of an unfair dismissal claim or an age discrimination claim.

However, this does not protect you against a finding of disability discrimination if Peter's condition is found to amount to a disability, and the dismissal is found to have been for a reason relating to Peter's disability.

Therefore, the company would be well advised to consider whether there are any adjustments it could make to allow Peter to carry on working –

Harry Sherrard

such as allowing someone else to climb ladders and allowing Peter his breaks. Alternatively, you could "retire" Peter and try to argue that it had nothing to do with his medical condition but rather was for some other reason – such as succession planning. There is no obligation on you to give reasons when turning down a request from an employee who wants to work on after retirement.

26

Question

Bill and Ben, employees at the same company, are both approaching 65. Bill has always been a model employee, Ben a problem. You decide to keep Bill on and retire Ben. Ben is furious, and threatens to go to tribunal due to this "blatant favouritism".

Can he?

Solution

Until 30th September 2011 under the Equality Act 2010, retiring an employee at 65 or over constitutes neither age discrimination nor unfair dismissal, as long as certain procedures are followed. Rather, it is a fair dismissal on the ground of retirement.

Provided the procedures are followed, this is true even where – as here – the retirement is clearly a sham and the real reason for the dismissal is something else altogether.

No reason for retirement need be given. So, although Ben might feel aggrieved, he cannot make a legal challenge.

Question

We run an outdoor pursuit company, and our employees are required to be extremely fit to undertake activities such as abseiling, kayaking, hiking with heavy equipment and so on. Patrick has now reached 60 and has noticeably slowed down over the last couple of years. Members of staff and customers have made observations to him about being a bit old for this kind of activity, which he has taken badly. He seems to have no intention of retiring. How do we handle this?

Solution

The current default retirement age is 65, and it is more or less impossible to justify an earlier retirement age. Even though this is a relatively extreme case with a lot of physical activity, the point holds good.

Therefore, the issue of age and retirement needs to be put to one side and the matter addressed by way of a capability procedure. Criteria and parameters need to be set, and if Patrick is not reaching these then a capability dismissal may result.

If Patrick claims age discrimination, the employer has two defences. First, that age is not a factor at all and that the matter has been handled purely on the basis of capability. Second, if Patrick succeeds in establishing that there were age related decisions made, the employer can seek to objectively justify the age discrimination. The employer will do this by demonstrating that the criteria and standards that it set are reasonable, and that it is objectively justified in dismissing older workers who fail to reach the necessary standards.

The employer will need proof that Patrick is working too slowly and that this dismissal is not based just on the perceptions of colleagues and customers.

Note that when compulsory retirement is abolished this kind of process will replace the existing retirement procedure. As a result, all employers should ensure that they have suitable and appropriate capability procedures in place.

Question

We have some staff aged over 65. Can we retire them in less than 6 months?

Solution

Currently, under the Equality Act 2010, retiring an employee at 65 or over constitutes neither age discrimination nor unfair dismissal, as long as certain procedures are followed. Generally, a 6 month procedure is followed (see page 23).

However, in this case you want to dismiss employees due to retirement with less than 6 months' notice. There is a shortened version of the statutory retirement procedure which employers can use to retire employees by giving only 14 days' notice of the intended date of retirement but be aware that, where short notice has been given, the employee can bring a claim for late notification, and will be entitled to an award of up to 8 weeks' pay (currently capped at £400 per week). In addition, the employee may have a claim for unfair dismissal as, by using the short procedure, it is not guaranteed that the dismissal will be deemed to be on the fair ground of retirement. Where the shortened procedure is used a tribunal can look beyond the reason for dismissal and, for example, where it finds that in reality retirement is being used as a way to dismiss an employee on capability grounds, the dismissal will be found to be unfair. This will not be a problem where the tribunal accepts that the reason for dismissal genuinely is retirement, but it will be a problem where retirement is being used as a facade for what is really a capability or misconduct dismissal (see page 28).

Question

Two employees have applied for promotion to a senior management position. They are both equally suited to the job but one of them lives with an elderly relative and frequently uses them as an excuse for lateness and absences from work.

What should you do?

Solution

The obvious answer from the company's point of view is to promote the employee without the caring responsibilities but this could mean you fall foul of discrimination legislation. Under the Equality Act 2010 direct discrimination claims based on association or perception are now allowed.

Age is a protected characteristic and so if your decision is based on the age of the employee's relative then you could be in trouble. However, if you base your decision on the caring responsibilities of the employee (carers are not protected from discrimination) then you should be fine. Provided that you can show that you treat all carers in the same way regardless of the age of the people they care for then they will not have a claim against you.

Would your answer be different if they had a pregnant wife and used her as an excuse?

No. You could still select the other employee for promotion. This is because employees cannot claim discrimination because of their association with someone who is pregnant. Generally speaking, as set out above, it is discrimination if you treat someone less favourably because of their association with someone who has a protected characteristic; however, this does not apply to marriage and civil partnership or pregnancy and maternity.

Question

Your best customer, Sharon, has been offending your entire workforce with her ageist comments. The other day she suggested that Tom, your 42 year old delivery driver, was too old to unload her stationery order from his van and that she would ask some of her 'young men' to give him a hand. He's thoroughly fed up and has complained to you about Sharon's behaviour.

What should you do?

Solution

Age is one of nine protected characteristics under the Equality Act 2010. Age harassment occurs when A engages in unwanted conduct that has the purpose or effect of violating B's dignity or creating an intimidating, hostile, degrading, humiliating or offensive environment for B.

If the conduct has the purpose of violating B's dignity then nothing more is required: this will amount to harassment. However, in this case it is unlikely that Sharon intended to harass Tom. Therefore, we have to look at whether her conduct nonetheless had the effect of violating his dignity. To some extent this is assessed from Tom's viewpoint and, when deciding how to respond, we will take into account that fact that Tom seems to have found the conduct offensive. However, we also need to consider whether it was reasonable for the conduct to have had this effect or whether Tom was being hypersensitive. In this case, we don't think that Tom was being hypersensitive but it is likely that a tribunal would think this was at the 'mild' end of the harassment spectrum.

Tom has been subjected to harassment by a third party; in this case your best customer. Are you liable? Under the Equality Act 2010 employers will be liable for third party harassment where the harassment a) takes place in the course of the employee's employment; b) the employer failed to take such steps as would have been reasonably practicable to prevent the third party from doing so; and c) the employer knew that the employee had been harassed by a third party on at least two other occasions.

It appears in this case that this is the first occasion on which Tom has complained to you so you are not liable. However, you should take action now to prevent this from happening again because, if you do nothing and the comments continue, Tom could have a claim against you. Reasonable steps could include having a tactful word with Sharon about her comments and asking her not to comment on Tom's age in the future. You obviously won't want to upset her as she is your best customer. A practical solution could also be to send a different delivery driver to Sharon's premises.

REDUNDANCY

Question

An estate agency firm with five branches needs to carry out a redundancy exercise. It is a very clear case of redundancy with a significant down-turn in business and an excess number of sales negotiators. There will be 30 redundancies in all. Faced with an urgent financial situation the redundancies have been announced abruptly, with employees being called into meetings to be informed of their redundancies with no previous warning.

What are the implications of these events?

Solution

Where you anticipate that there will be 20 or more redundancies at one establishment within a 30 day period then collective rules apply. Here the redundancies are spread across five branches and, although it is all one company with one management structure, it is nonetheless the case that each of the five branches will constitute a separate establishment. Therefore there is no requirement to undertake collective consultation. Where there is a requirement to undertake collective consultation and this is not done, the employer can face a penalty of 90 days' pay per employee affected. This is based on actual pay and not the statutory cap (currently £400).

Irrespective of the fact that the collective rules do not apply in this case, it is likely that these dismissals were unfair. Unfair dismissal law requires an employer to inform and consult with individual members of staff, select on a fair basis and consider alternative employment. It seems that there was minimal regard for these issues in carrying out in these redundancies, which would result in a tribunal finding that they were unfair dismissals.

With regard to compensation, the case of Polkey is important here. This case was a House of Lords decision. Under this authority, if employees who have been unfairly dismissed would in any event have been fairly dismissed within a short period of time if a proper procedure had been followed, compensation is limited to the period during which that procedure should have been taking place. In a situation such as this, the estate agency firm can point to the urgent financial pressures that it was under and would be able to make a credible case that a proper consultation process, with proper selection and followed by an appeal, would have taken about, say, four weeks. If the tribunal is convinced by that argument, it has the ability to limit an award to four weeks' earnings per employee.

Note that the Polkey principle will only apply if the tribunal is satisfied that the dismissals were inevitable and were unfair only due to being rushed and with inadequate consultation and procedures. If an employee were able to demonstrate, for example, that he or she has certain qualifications that would have lead to them not being selected for redundancy if the employer had given proper consideration to the matter, Polkey will not serve to limit compensation. Employees in this category can receive an award up to £68,400 by way of a compensatory award.

Question

A nursery employs a lot of seasonal staff, with the same people coming back year on year. The seasonal staff work from September to June and have July and August off. The nursery now wants to make some redundancies. Will they have to pay these seasonal staff statutory redundancy?

Solution

An employee is entitled to a statutory redundancy payment if they can show two (calendar) years' continuous employment under s155 of the Employment Rights Act 1996 ("the ERA").

The issue that needs to be considered here is whether or not the seasonal staff would be able to show that their employment has been continuous despite the fact that they did not work during two months each summer. The rules on this are set out in sections 210 to 219 of the Act. Under section 210(5), there is a presumption in favour of the employee that any period of employment is continuous. The onus is therefore on the employer to prove that the employment was not continuous.

Employment will not be continuous where there is a break in employment. For the purposes of the ERA, a week that does not count in computing the length of an employee's period of continuous employment breaks continuity of employment (section 253(1)). Under the Act, a week which breaks continuity runs from Saturday to Sunday. A week's break in employment must therefore be a week with two weekends either side. Applying this practically, it is usually best to consider whether there have been two full weeks' break in employment.

However, weeks where there is a contract of employment count as weeks of continuous employment under section 212(1) of the Act even if the employee is not actually at work. Here, the nursery staff clearly have contracts running from September to June, and this would most certainly be a period of continuous employment. However, even if they have no contract over the summer months, this still might be counted as continuous employment under the Act. Section 212 sets out circumstances where continuity of employment is preserved during an interval between two contracts of employment.

Under s212(3)(b) continuity will be preserved where an employee is absent from work as a result of temporary cessation of work. In the nursery, there is an interval where there is no work due to the summer break. There is no limit to the length of this interval, and so two months' summer holiday would indeed fall under this section, and continuity of employment would not be broken.

The work for the seasonal staff in the nursery stops over the summer when the children are on holiday, and resumes in September when they return. This is clearly a temporary cessation of work and so the staffs' employment is continuous, notwithstanding their two-month summer break each year.

Furthermore, under s212(3)(c), continuity will be preserved where an employee is absent from work in circumstances where, by arrangement or custom, they are regarded as continuing in employment. If the staff are leaving for the summer, and both they and the employer have the intention for them to return in September, this could be seen as such an arrangement. This seems very likely to be the case in these circumstances as the same staff return "year on year". This again, would mean that continuity would not be broken.

Taking the above into account, it seems that the seasonal staff will be entitled to statutory redundancy pay, provided that they started working at the nursery over two years ago.

Question

A secretary has been working part-time for some years, but the requirements have increased and it is now a full time job. She has refused to go onto full time hours.

How does the employer handle this?

Solution

The employer has a choice of two approaches. Either this can be dealt with as a restructure, in which case if it dismisses the part time member of staff and replaces her with a full time member of staff the dismissal will be for "some other substantial reason", or the employer can treat it as a redundancy situation.

Although redundancy is usually considered in the context of reducing requirements for work, rather than an overall increase, it is nonetheless arguable that the part time secretarial position is now redundant. Redundancy is defined as being a reduction in the employer's requirements for "work of a particular kind", and the part time position can be regarded as coming under this definition. Therefore the employer should go through a redundancy process but offer the full time position as an alternative. If the employee does not accept the alternative, then statutory redundancy pay needs to be paid, or company redundancy pay if there is a company redundancy scheme.

The alternative, but slightly higher risk approach, is not to pay redundancy but to treat this as a restructure, in which case the employer will put forward the alternative fair reason for dismissal of "some other substantial reason". The substantial reason in this case would be simply that the employer now has a greater amount of work to do and its position that it requires a full timer is therefore justified. In these circumstances no statutory or other redundancy pay would be payable, but this is likely to result in a more disgruntled member of staff and an increased likelihood of an unfair dismissal claim.

There is some possibility of a sex discrimination angle in this case as well. If the secretary is the mother of young children, and wishes to work part time to care for them, it may be unlawful indirect sex discrimination to place a requirement on her to work full time. In those circumstances the employer should consider two part time job share positions or other flexible alternatives to avoid an allegation of sex discrimination. If, however, the secretary does not have small children then the mere fact that she is a female does not give rise to a potential sex discrimination claim.

Question

We are consulting with our IT Manager concerning a possible redundancy. The IT Manager has a reputation for being disruptive and rather anti-company, and we are worried that he may do some damage to the IT systems during the consultation period. Can we put him on garden leave during the consultation process?

Solution

It is a common misconception that garden leave can be triggered at any time. In order to put someone on garden leave you must have an express clause in the employee's contract of employment and, usually, garden leave clauses are worded so that they only can be operated during the notice period, and therefore cannot be triggered until notice has been served either by the employer or the employee. Consequently, in most cases the answer to this question will be no – the employee cannot be put on garden leave as he had not yet been given notice, as at this stage you are still consulting with him about a possible redundancy situation.

Whilst putting the employee on garden leave is not possible, you could still ask him to agree to a period of additional paid leave, and you must continue to consult with him whilst he is on paid leave.

If the employee refuses to agree to a period of paid leave, you could take the more drastic step of suspending him; however, in most cases this is inadvisable as it could open the door for the employee to resign in response to being suspended for (as he would see it) no good reason, and bring a constructive unfair dismissal claim. Such a claim would not necessarily succeed as it would be a question of fact and degree in the particular case but nonetheless the better option would be to agree with the employee that he take a period of paid leave.

Question

We are carrying out redundancies, and an employee is on maternity leave. Some of the financial selection criteria we have had to estimate, as there are no recent figures. We've given the employee on maternity leave a high assumed score. Is this likely to lead to any problems?

Solution

This could cause a problem if the female employee is in a selection pool with a male colleague, and whilst the female employee is receiving the highest score possible under a selection criterion the male's scores are lower because his actual figures are being relied on. If the scores under that particular criterion were decisive, and lead to the male receiving the lowest score overall and being made redundant instead of his female colleague who is on maternity leave, the male could bring a direct sex discrimination claim and an unfair dismissal claim.

This happened in the case of De Belin v Eversheds Legal Services Ltd, where a female lawyer was given an artificially high score under a particular selection criterion because she did not have any actual figures that could be used as she had been absent on maternity leave. Her male colleague was given a score based on his actual figures. The male employee received the lowest score overall and was made redundant but as the difference between the employees score was a mere $\frac{1}{2}$ point, the artificial score that the female employee had received had been decisive.

The selection criteria applied was held to be sex discrimination and the employee's dismissal was found to be unfair. The tribunal found that, whilst it was not possible for Eversheds to give the female lawyer an actual score for the period that she was absent due to maternity leave, it could have disregarded the score altogether or used a different reference period.

If the employee who is on maternity leave is in a pool with other female colleagues who are not on maternity leave they could not, however, bring direct sex discrimination claims in the same circumstances. This is because they would not be able to say that they were being treated differently to a male comparator, as the comparator would be another female. This would not necessarily prevent the female employees bringing an unfair dismissal claim on the basis that the selection criterion has been applied unfairly.

It is important for employers to remember that in a redundancy situation involving a woman on maternity leave the only way in which the female employee should receive more favourable treatment is in relation to suitable alternative vacancies. This is because a female employee whose job becomes redundant during her maternity leave is entitled to be offered any suitable alternative vacancy that exists with her employer. In all other regards the employer should treat the female employee on maternity leave in the same way that it treats other employees in a redundancy situation.

Question

We were just about to tell an employee that she is in a pool of people at risk of redundancy when she told us that she is pregnant. There may be alternative vacancies. Should we proceed, and if so, how?

Solution

An employee who is made redundant whilst on maternity leave has an automatic right to be offered any suitable vacancy within the company. In effect, such a person jumps the queue ahead of other more suitable candidates, should that be the situation. However, this employee is currently pregnant and not yet on maternity leave. The automatic right to the alternative vacancy does not arise as a result of pregnancy. Therefore, for the time being, you should carry on the process as you had been, scoring the employees on a fair and objective basis. Remember that if the selection criteria includes attendance, any pregnancy related absence – for example ante-natal classes or doctor's appointments – should be disregarded in the pregnant employee's score to avoid any potential claim for sex discrimination. The redundancy programme began before the employee announced her pregnancy, and it should therefore not impact the process. Depending on timing, if the employee does then go on maternity leave before the redundancy is complete, and there are vacancies, she has the entitlement to be offered those alternative roles as explained above.

Question

Your south-east sales manager, Laura, is currently on maternity leave. She is due to return next month and has indicated that she would like to cut down from five to four days a week.

Unfortunately the south east region has not been successful under Laura. She is aware of this but has not been formally spoken to. The MD has decided that the south east region needs an area manager (dealing with purchasing, stock control and client relations as well as just sales) and doesn't think Laura is the right person. The view is that she lacks flair and that her skills are more suited to straight selling. The new role will also be a full time role based in the London head office and will require extensive travel – whereas the old role was based mainly in Sussex near Laura's home.

The company could offer Laura a new sales role based in Brighton but it would be a more junior position, not on the management team, and on a lower salary.

Can they say Laura's old role is redundant and offer her the new Brighton-based sales role?

Solution

If you have decided that the job needs to be done full-time from London then you could argue that the job of working around Sussex is becoming redundant. You would always face the risk of Laura saying that the decision was related to the fact that she was returning from maternity leave (and therefore constituted less favourable treatment relating to her maternity) so you would have to be very sure of your grounds for doing this.

The fact that Laura herself was underperforming would not be grounds for making her role redundant. It might be grounds for terminating her employment/changing her job role on the grounds of capability but this would be a more drawn-out process – particularly in light of the fact that she is only just returning from maternity leave.

Therefore, you will need "non-Laura-related" reasons for deciding that you want the job to be done full time from London and with more travelling.

But that is only the start of it.... If Laura's existing role is made redundant, you are under an obligation to consider her for any suitable alternative vacancies.

If her role is made redundant while she is away on maternity leave, she is entitled not only to be considered for any suitable alternative vacancy; she is entitled to be offered any suitable alternative vacancy. The job you are proposing to create (of London-based area manager with some travel) would, potentially, be a suitable alternative vacancy for Laura. We might say "we don't think Laura would be suitable for that job as we don't think she's up to it" but - from a legal point of view - that's not the point. If the job is suitable for Laura (and, bearing in mind she's been doing a job much like it for some time and no-one's ever formally addressed her failings in the role) then Laura is entitled to be offered the job.

If the decision to make Laura's existing role redundant is made after she returns from maternity, she is entitled to apply for and be considered for the role. You are not under the same obligation to simply offer it to Laura (once she is back from maternity leave, she loses that extra level of protection) but, for the reasons set out above, you could still face very strong claims for unfair dismissal and sex discrimination if we don't offer Laura the London-based role if she wants it.

So, the "redundancy" idea is unlikely to work here.

What we could do is explain to Laura that we have restructured her role and there are now two roles; the first is the London-based area manager role with lots of travel and the second is the Brighton-based role with no travel. If Laura is prepared to accept the latter, then there is no problem. Bearing in mind the fact that she has already asked for her hours to be cut down, she might go for that. But, if she calls our bluff and states a preference for the London role, we could well be stuck (from a legal point of view) with having to give her a chance. We might turn down the inevitable flexible working request but - if she's still prepared to try the London role - we'll have to give her a chance.

Alternatively, we could have an entirely open discussion with her on a without-prejudice basis and offer her a termination payment to go. We could warn that - if she takes up the London role - we will be watching her very carefully and possibly commencing some sort of performance review process. In the circumstances, she might prefer to leave with a sum of money.

So, in conclusion, the first step is to explain the restructure plan (and the reasons for that restructure plan) to Laura and try - in the most careful way possible - to sell the Brighton role to her. In doing so, we will have to be careful not to suggest that we think her childcare responsibilities will get in the way of her doing the London job - that will be something for her to decide for herself. We should explain that the London job is hers if she wants it - although we can explain (in an entirely neutral way) that it will involve travel. If she doesn't accept that and states instead a preference to go for the London job, we will either have to grit our teeth and bear it or commence without prejudice discussions with her. She might be prepared to take the Brighton job if she can have a compensation payment as well to compensate her for the fact that she will be losing her senior job and salary.

Question

Angela and Tracey both work full time for Tripaway as travel consultants. Angela holds the managerial position.

A recent downturn in business has meant that Tripaway need to reduce the headcount in the department from 2 to 1.5. As a result, Tripaway have offered Tracey a new job which is 50% in travel and 50% in administration. Although Tracey has never worked in administration before the company is confident that, with the right training and guidance, she will easily be able to pick the job up.

Upon consideration, Tracey declined the job offer and said that she only wanted to work as a travel consultant. She said that she would be happy to accept a part time role in travel instead and be available for cover during vacation and sick leave period.

Tracey then asked if she was eligible for financial compensation as she felt that, whilst it is her choice to remain at Tripaway and accept a part time job, it is in fact being imposed on her by the company.

Is Tracey entitled to financial compensation?

Solution

If Tracey just agreed to a reduction in hours, then that could be considered a variation in contract, however, that is not the position here. As Tripaway are reducing their staff from 2 to 1.5, and making Tracey's full time role redundant, this makes it a redundancy situation.

In a redundancy situation, the employer has an obligation to consider suitable alternatives. Tripaway have achieved this by offering Tracey the 50% travel and 50% administration role. Where an employee unreasonably turns down a suitable alternative position, he/she loses the right to statutory redundancy pay. However, it is relatively easy for the employee to assert that the alternative is not suitable and/or that he/she was not unreasonable in turning it down. In this situation, Tracey is therefore entitled to turn down the suggested alternative role and revert to redundancy if she so wished.

However, Tracey has expressed that she does not want to leave Tripaway and instead has said she will work part time instead of full time in the travel department. Although it may seem a little unfair, if an employee accepts any alternative position, even one that is not strictly speaking "suitable", then he/she loses their entitlement to redundancy pay.

Therefore, by Tracey accepting her new role, she loses her entitlement to statutory redundancy. Of course, the company could give her some sort of discretional financial compensation if it chose. Indeed it could pay her statutory redundancy on a voluntary basis, and explain to Tracey that her redundancy pay clock would thereby be re-set at zero. In any future redundancy exercise, her entitlement would be counted from the start of her role in the part time job, and not from the commencement of employment.

DISCIPLINARY, DISMISSAL AND GRIEVANCES

Question

An employee has been off sick and a "friend" of hers in the workplace has shown us her entries on Facebook which reveal that she has been on holiday and participating in social activities and she does not seem to be ill. Can we use the Facebook evidence in a disciplinary process with a view to dismissing her? If we do this and she brings a tribunal claim will the Facebook evidence be admissible in the tribunal?

Solution

In relation to the first question, can we use the Facebook evidence in a disciplinary with a view to dismissing this employee, we recommend that employers do use this information.

An employer is entitled to use evidence against an employee that comes to its attention through information she has made publicly available through Facebook, in circumstances where the employer is informed about the information on Facebook by another employee who is 'friends' with the employee on Facebook.

In the normal way, the employer needs to present the evidence to employees in a disciplinary context, listen to the answers/explanations given and then make a decision. Evidence obtained from Facebook is no different to evidence obtained from other sources.

If this employee is dismissed and brings an unfair dismissal claim she could potentially argue that in obtaining the information the employer has acted in breach of Article 8 of the Human Rights Act ('HRA') – the right to respect for private and family life. The HRA has direct effect only on public sector organisations. Assuming therefore that this is a private sector employer, the HRA will not apply. The HRA nonetheless has an impact in tribunal proceedings. The tribunal is in the public sector and is bound by section 6 of the HRA not to act in a way that is incompatible with a Convention right.

If a tribunal believes that evidence has been obtained which is in breach of the HRA, it can make an order that this evidence is disregarded. This would occur at a pre hearing review, before the main hearing. Since in this particular case the disciplinary and subsequent dismissal seems largely to rest on the information posted on Facebook, if the employer is not allowed to use that information, the effect of such a decision by the tribunal would be to strike out their defence and the employee would in effect win by default.

However, any attempt to argue a right to privacy is unlikely to succeed where an employee has put information onto Facebook because, by doing so, the employee is effectively publishing the information and that is how it has come to the employer's attention, via a third party, the employee's 'friend'.

In any event, even if such an argument could get past this first hurdle, the right to privacy afforded by Article 8 is not absolute. It competes against other articles and, importantly in this case, Article 6 (the right to a fair trial). It is highly likely that this competing right will be deemed more important than the right to respect for private and family life and that therefore the evidence will be allowed. Further, breach of the right to a private and family life can also be justified where this is done '...for the prevention of disorder or crime' and in this case fraudulently claiming sick pay is arguably a criminal offence and therefore derogation from the right to privacy may be justifiable in order to prevent a criminal activity.

So, although it is theoretically possible that a tribunal could refuse to admit evidence obtained in breach of privacy, it would be highly unlikely in this case.

Question

Can we dismiss staff for criticising the company on Facebook?

Solution

There are two aspects to this. First, is accessing an employee's Facebook page a breach of their right to privacy (in which case would it be dangerous for the company to rely on information provided on Facebook to justify disciplinary action)? The second is the issue of the employee broadcasting criticism about the company through Facebook and whether this justifies dismissal.

In relation to the first point, if an employer obtains information about an employee through information he/she has put on his Facebook the employer is generally entitled to rely on this information to justify taking disciplinary action (see page 51).

The second question is whether criticising the company on Facebook is serious enough to justify dismissal, and the linked issue of distribution of information about the company through Facebook. Whilst it is probably unrealistic to expect that employees will never criticise the company, the fact that these criticisms appear on Facebook does give the complaint an additional dimension. The criticism is being more widely distributed and potentially does have a harmful effect on the company's reputation. It comes down to how severe the criticism is, and whether in fact the company's reputation has been harmed. In a serious case a dismissal could be justified, but it is probably more likely to result in a warning in most cases.

Given the increasing use of social networking sites such as Facebook employers would be well advised to implement a social networking site policy to ensure, in particular, that they cover the consequences of making derogatory comments or postings about the employer on social networking sites.

Question

An employee has written a blog, seen by many people, criticising the company and its management.

Can we dismiss him?

Solution

Whether this employee can be fairly dismissed comes down to the seriousness of the comments that have been made.

Generally speaking, tribunals are reluctant to use "bringing the employer into disrepute" as a sufficient reason to dismiss. It can be an area that the employer feels very strongly about, but can the employer really say that the ramblings of a junior member of staff who clearly has some kind of grudge will be taken seriously by the public, and will in fact damage the reputation of the employer?

As well as the seriousness of the remarks, whether or not these could be fair dismissals is influenced by the seniority of the staff involved. Clearly if a more senior member of staff with management responsibilities makes these kinds of criticisms, that would be viewed much more seriously than similar criticisms from a junior member of staff.

If the employer can show that an employee has wilfully and maliciously set out to harm the employer's business by publishing allegations that he or she knew, or should reasonably have known, to be false, then this is likely to be serious enough to justify dismissal.

The employer is well advised to cover blogs in the social networking site policy (see page 53). If the employer has said that blogs must not contain information about the business, disciplinary action is much easier to justify.

Question

One of your secretaries, Barbara, has shown herself to be lazy and incompetent. She has been with you for 5 years and the issue has not been properly addressed throughout that time. The MD says that he wants her out and it must happen within a week.

What can you do to minimise the risks?

Solution

Barbara has never been advised that there were concerns about her performance. As such, the issues have not been recorded at any appraisals and Barbara has never been put on a performance improvement plan. To dismiss Barbara now without following any kind of procedures will undoubtedly be unfair.

In order for a dismissal to be fair, you must consider the "reasonableness" principles. In a capability procedure, this involves providing the employee with training, warning him or her the improvement is required, and giving him or her a chance to improve. The timescale here means that it is highly unlikely that the dismissal will be fair.

The best way to minimise the risks to the company would be to offer Barbara a compromise agreement.

The procedure for this is as follows:

You should give Barbara a letter, notifying her of the allegations of poor performance and inviting her to a meeting to discuss the matter. You (or, preferably, someone else in the organisation) will then have an "off the record" discussion with Barbara and explain that, as an alternative to going through the disciplinary procedure, the company is offering an ex-gratia payment under a compromise agreement.

If Barbara is interested in this option, she will seek legal advice and hopefully sign the compromise agreement.

If she refuses or drags her feet about the terms of the compromise agreement, you will then proceed to have the disciplinary meeting.

By giving her the letter prior to the "without prejudice" discussion the company will:

(a)   have a valid dispute to discuss with Barbara 'off the record';

(b)   show Barbara's legal advisor that the company is intending to follow a fair disciplinary procedure;

(c)   retain an "escape route" if Barbara refuses to sign the compromise agreement

What about just giving Barbara the draft agreement with no letter first? The danger here is that if you do not have a "dispute" to resolve, the compromise agreement is not considered to be "without prejudice" and can be produced by Barbara in a tribunal, which would be embarrassing and damaging to an already weak position. This letter is therefore an important safeguard.

With regard to the amount to offer Barbara in the agreement, as a secretary she is likely to be in a position to mitigate her loss fairly quickly. So a payment of about 3 months' salary would be a reasonable offer, but if she argues for a lot more you may need to obtain information about alternative vacancies in the locality to demonstrate that she had not taken all reasonable steps to mitigate her loss.

Question

Jim, a photocopier repair engineer with 15 years' unblemished service with your company, has made two or three silly mistakes over the last few months – such as spilling toner all over the carpet at one client's offices and causing a three-hour power-cut at another client's offices by forgetting to unplug a machine he was working on. Those two clients make up 90% of the work in the region Jim covers and both clients have said they no longer want Jim to do their work.

Can you dismiss Jim for misconduct/capability/anything else?

Solution

As Jim has an unblemished record until the last few months, if we want to terminate his employment on the grounds of conduct, we will have to be able to argue that his acts of misconduct were so serious as to amount to gross misconduct. There is no indication here that he carried out these acts deliberately and therefore a conduct dismissal is unlikely to succeed in tribunal.

Dismissing an employee fairly on the grounds of capability for a single act of negligence or incompetence is rare. Here, while there have been a number of issues over the last few months, nothing has been done about them. Generally, incapability is established over a longer period of time during which the employee receives warnings and assistance to help him improve. A single act of incompetence can lead to a fair dismissal in situations where that act undermines the employer's confidence in the employee, but generally that only applies in situations where the mistake could have a "calamitous" effect. The sort of mistakes which have led to fair dismissals are mistakes which put people's lives at risk (for example a pilot landing a plane negligently and a mechanic failing to ensure that a new car was safe to drive before allowing it off the forecourt). Mistakes which are costly but not dangerous do not generally lead to fair dismissals on the grounds of capability.

This situation could lead to a fair dismissal on the grounds of "third party pressure to dismiss" – which is one of the fair grounds under "Some Other Substantial Reason".

In order to carry out this sort of dismissal, the company will need to show that the two clients issued some sort of ultimatum – "take Jim away from our contract or we will withdraw the contract". If we can get this in writing from the clients, we will be more likely to succeed.

In the case of Greenwood v Whiteghyll Plastics Limited (2007) the Employment Appeal Tribunal reminded employers that, where they are considering dismissing an employee as a result of pressure from a third party such as one of the employer's clients, they must consider whether (and to what extent) there would be any injustice to the employee as a result of being dismissed. If they conclude that injustice would result, they must also consider any steps that could be taken to alleviate that injustice.

In this case, Jim has worked for the company for a long time. We will probably need to be able to show that we at least carried out our own investigations into the clients' reasons for wanting Jim off their contracts. We will also have to consider what – if any – roles Jim could do which would not require him to work with those clients. Subject to those considerations, though, we could dismiss Jim fairly.

It is worth noting that in these sorts of claims dismissals are more likely to be fair if an employee has been warned that they might be dismissed if a client places pressure on you to do so – perhaps something that should be added to contracts of employment if you have employees who work on client sites or whose work is mostly for one or two clients.

Question

An employee, whom we believed, was guilty of quite serious misconduct was dismissed. He has brought a tribunal claim and, in reviewing the case now, it's our view that there were some significant procedural defects in the disciplinary procedure. If we lose the case on procedure, but the tribunal accepts that the misconduct did take place, where would this leave us?

Solution

Whilst there would still be a finding of unfair dismissal against the employer, the fact that the tribunal accepts that the misconduct did take place should have a bearing on the amount of compensation the tribunal awards to the employee.

In unfair dismissal cases where the Claimant is successful there are two main awards a tribunal can make: the basic award and the compensatory award.

The basic award is calculated in the same way as a redundancy payment. Consequently, an employee who is successful in an unfair dismissal claim will receive one week's pay (capped at £400) for each complete year of employment (up to a maximum of 20 weeks).

The compensatory award is essentially an award for loss of earnings for however long the tribunal decide it is reasonable for an employee to take to find new employment. The maximum is currently £68,400 but typically awards for loss of earnings are in the region of 6 months' salary, although this does vary. A Claimant does have a duty to mitigate his losses and to find new employment. If he finds new employment he will not receive any further award for loss of earnings after that point (save for any difference between his old and new earnings). Where the employee has not found new employment or has taken a long time to find new employment, the employer can produce evidence at the hearing, such as advertisements for vacancies that the Claimant could have applied for. If the tribunal is convinced that the Claimant has not done enough to find new employment it will limit the compensatory award to a period within which the panel believes the Claimant could have found new employment.

Once a tribunal has decided how much to award the Claimant under these headings the tribunal can make further deductions to reduce the amount that the Claimant will receive where there is some wrongdoing on the part of the Claimant:

Polkey Deduction

First of all, the tribunal can apply what is known as a Polkey Deduction to the compensatory award – this is a reduction based on the possibility that the Claimant would have been dismissed in any event, and that as such the procedural defects made no real difference to the outcome. The tribunal can reduce an award on this basis by any amount it considers to be just and equitable. Where the tribunal finds that had proper procedures been followed the dismissal still would have happened but would have been delayed, the tribunal can apply a Polkey Deduction so that the compensatory award will reflect the period during which the Claimant would have remained in employment while the proper procedure was being followed. It is also possible for a tribunal to find that, despite the fact that the dismissal was unfair, the employee would have been fairly dismissed for another reason shortly afterwards in any event. Accordingly it can reduce the compensation to the Claimant to reflect that possibility.

Contributory fault

Secondly, the tribunal can also apply a reduction on account of contributory fault. A reduction for contributory fault can affect both the basic award and the compensatory award and can result in an award for compensation being reduced by up to 100%, in which case, despite there being a finding of unfair dismissal, the employee will leave the tribunal with no compensation.

Question

One of your employees, Victor, uses the company phone to make an expensive personal phone call to his mother in Spain. Whilst this is a serious act of misconduct, having investigated the matter, you do not believe that Victor's actions can be said to amount to an act of gross misconduct. Nonetheless you do believe that dismissal is a reasonable sanction to impose.

If you dismiss Victor is he likely to win an unfair dismissal claim?

Solution

In order to defeat the claim you need to show that you had a genuine belief that the employee had committed the act of misconduct founded upon a reasonable investigation. You would then have to demonstrate that in dismissing Victor for that reason you acted within the band of reasonable responses.

If the tribunal panel hearing the case accepts that your actions in dismissing Victor were within the range of reasonable responses you should be able to defeat his claim. This remains the case even if the tribunal agree with you that Victor's actions did not amount to gross misconduct entitling you to dismiss Victor without notice. Misconduct that falls short of gross misconduct may still be serious enough to justify dismissal and thereby make the dismissal fair. This point has recently been reiterated in a case that went to the Employment Appeal Tribunal – Weston Recovery Service v Fisher 2010. In this case an employee's actions in returning a company vehicle he had borrowed, with the consent of his employer for a holiday to France, in an unsafe condition were deemed to amount to serious misconduct entitling his employers to dismiss him even though they fell short of gross misconduct. Overturning the tribunal's decision to hold that the dismissal was unfair, the EAT held that, even though the dismissal was not as a result of an act of gross misconduct, it was nonetheless a fair dismissal because it was within the band of reasonable responses. It is a common misconception that dismissal is only ever reasonable in response to an act of gross misconduct.

Where Victor may succeed at tribunal is if you fail to pay him for his notice period. In these circumstances, whilst he would lose his unfair dismissal claim because dismissal was within the band of reasonable responses, he would succeed in a wrongful dismissal claim. This is a claim an employee can bring when an employer has failed to pay an employee for his notice period. The reason the employee would succeed is because it is only when the employee has committed an act of gross misconduct that you do not have to pay the employee for his notice period. Here, as the employee's actions fell short of gross misconduct, you should have either let him work out his notice period or paid him in lieu of his notice period. If the employee does bring a wrongful dismissal claim the compensation he will receive will be his notice pay, and nothing else.

Question

An employee who is facing a disciplinary hearing has put in a subject access request and has specifically asked for 'all emails and other written communications between my departmental manager and the HR Department'. On investigation we have discovered that there were a number of emails saying highly uncomplimentary things about him that were sent by the manager to HR. Do we need to disclose these, and what might the penalty be if we do not?

Solution

A subject access request is a request by an employee made under the Data Protection Act 1998 for personal information his or her employer processes about the employee.

The Data Protection Act does not give the data subject (the employee) the right to have, or even to inspect, a copy of documents containing personal data. Rather, the employee making a subject access request simply has the right to be informed in writing of what personal data the data controller holds about him/her. In practice, rather than extracting such data from a file so that it can be given to the individual, it will often be easier to let the employee inspect the file.

In terms of what data needs to be provided, under the Data Protection Act only personal data need be provided. This has been interpreted by the courts to mean information that is 'biographical in a significant sense' and which has the individual as its focus. Consequently, any emails between the departmental manager and the HR Department which do not contain biographical information about this employee do not need to be disclosed. For example, an email listing employees attending a course which includes this employee's name will not need to be disclosed.

However, data which expresses any opinion about this employee is likely to fall within the definition of personal data and, as such, the uncomplimentary emails sent by the manager to HR about this employee should be disclosed.

If the employee subsequently brings a case in a tribunal these documents will most likely need to be disclosed in any event. A solicitor has a legal duty to disclose documentation that he or she knows about even if that information is unfavourable to his or her client's case. In view of this it is good practice to train managers not to make uncomplimentary comments about employees in emails or other written correspondence and make them aware of the scope for disclosure of such documents both under the Data Protection Act and in connection with tribunal proceedings.

If the employer refuses to fully comply with the employee's subject access request, the employee can make a request to the Information Commissioner asking the Commissioner to determine whether or not it is likely that the subject access request has been carried out lawfully. The Commissioner is under a duty to make an assessment and serve notice on an employer requiring it to give him the information. The employee may also make an application to court alleging breach of the data subject access request and seek an order for compliance and/or damages. An employer should be able to defend a claim for damages if it can show that it had taken such steps as were reasonable in the circumstances to comply with the subject access request.

Consequently, an employer should take the following action points into consideration when dealing with a subject access request:

1. It is advisable to appoint someone to be responsible for overseeing the collation of the relevant data. If someone in the company has been appointed as the data protection manager they could assume this responsibility.

2. Information requested under the Data Protection Act needs to be provided within 40 days. It is a good idea to inform all staff involved in obtaining and collating this information of the timescale.

3. Under the Data Protection Act, as there is no obligation to provide actual documents (for example, a letter or an email) containing personal data only the information constituting the personal data contained in the document, rather than copying/printing documents that you have you can simply put the data you have on a memory stick or CD.

4. You must make sure that any information disclosed to the employee making the data subject request does not result in disclosure of information relating to another individual and, consequently, you may need to redact or delete names of other parties from any documents or alternatively seek the third party's consent before information is disclosed to the other employee.

5. It is advisable to keep a record of the method you have followed in searching for the data. See also page 138.

Question

Alf has been accused of fiddling his expenses. The disciplinary meeting found Alf guilty and he was given a written warning. You are hearing Alf's appeal and you think the sanction was pretty light and that he should have been dismissed.

What can you do?

Solution

Some disciplinary procedures allow employers to increase sanctions at appeal. Indeed, it is a sensible provision to put into a disciplinary procedure – as the employee will have absolutely nothing to lose by appealing if the employer is not able to increase the sanction at appeal. It could also be helpful where new evidence had come to light since the original hearing – making a harsher sanction more appropriate.

Without an express clause in the disciplinary procedure, however, we do not recommend increasing sanction at appeal.

Question

Jasper is being disciplined for insubordination to his manager, George, and rudeness to customers. He has been suspended. The disciplinary will be heard by Marcus, the regional manager. The day before the disciplinary is due to take place, Jasper sends in a grievance letter, alleging that George has been bullying him.

What do you do?

Solution

It is a common misconception that grievances and disciplinaries always need to be separated. It is generally inappropriate to hold a separate grievance process when the grievance relates to the disciplinary matter.

Indeed, the ACAS Code of Practice on Disciplinary and Grievance procedures in paragraph 44 provides that where disciplinary and grievance cases are related, the issues can be dealt with concurrently. Here, as the grievance and the disciplinary issue seem to be related, you should be able to deal with both matters at once. But do ensure that Jasper's grievance is given proper consideration and investigated and discussed at the meeting.

Is your answer different if Jasper alleges that the reason that George bullied him is that Jasper is gay and George is homophobic?

This is still the case if Jasper is alleging that the reason that George bullied him is because Jasper is gay. Even though there is a discrimination allegation, that allegation is still directly related to the disciplinary allegations, and so can be dealt with concurrently.

If the evidence you find means that you uphold the grievance Jasper has raised you would need to take action against George (by going through a disciplinary procedure with him) but that does not mean that you cannot continue with the conduct disciplinary against Jasper if it is deserved.

Question

An employee who works shifts has come into the company whilst not on duty, smelling strongly of alcohol and clearly inebriated. Our contracts state that being under the influence of alcohol whilst at work is gross misconduct, but is it gross misconduct if the employee attended work outside of his normal working hours?

Solution

Probably not. The purpose of the gross misconduct rule in the contract is to prevent the employee from potentially discharging duties whilst intoxicated. Here, whilst being a nuisance, the employee was not actually attempting to discharge duties. It is probably worth some disciplinary action such as a written warning, but a one off instance of this behaviour is unlikely to justify dismissal.

The event may alert the employer to an alcohol problem. All employers are highly recommended to have drug and alcohol testing abilities in their contracts. The drug and alcohol testing policy should provide that testing can be carried out either randomly or on suspicion. Given this event, it would be reasonable to ask the employee to undertake an alcohol test at some point in the future if there was some level of suspicion that he was again under the influence of alcohol.

Question

One of your employees has been arrested and charged with being drunk on an aircraft, hitting a fellow passenger and assaulting a member of the cabin crew. He is due to stand trial next month and is planning to plead guilty. A prison sentence is inevitable.

His solicitor has written to you asking you to provide a character reference to be used in mitigation at his trial...

You are appalled by this employee's behaviour. You are also worried that, as yours is a fairly high profile company and "air-rage" is a favourite topic of the press, this case may bring some adverse publicity for your company. Far from providing a character reference, you would rather sack him.

What can you do?

Solution

You are certainly not obliged to provide a character reference for this employee.

However, as far as disciplinary procedures go, the situation is very different from the situation where a crime has been committed in the workplace. Tribunals and courts have been critical in the past of employers who automatically dismiss their employees because of crimes they have committed outside the workplace.

The main guidance for employers on the issue of criminal charges or convictions outside employment is found in the ACAS Code of Practice on Disciplinary & Grievance Procedures. This states that "if any employee is charged with, or convicted of a criminal offence this is not normally in itself reason for disciplinary action. Consideration needs to be given to what effect the charge or conviction has on the employee's suitability, to do the job and their relationship with their employer, work colleagues and customers."

Case law suggests that worries over adverse publicity are insufficient grounds for dismissing an employee. While adverse publicity relating to this employee's court case would be unwelcome, it would be hard to prove that it would directly affect your business, for example, in terms of sales.

Examples of cases where it has been successfully argued that a crime performed outside the workplace affected an employer's business interests include a shop security guard who was convicted of shoplifting and a railway worker who was convicted of assaulting a member of the British Transport Police.

If the employee is given a lengthy prison sentence, it could effectively 'frustrate' the contract of employment, however, how 'lengthy' a prison sentence needs to be in order to frustrate a contract of employment is not entirely clear. Sentences of 12 months or more have been held in the past to be sufficiently 'lengthy' to frustrate contracts of employment, so in general it is best to assume that a shorter sentence will not end the contract. That does not mean that it is not possible to dismiss, but you should only do so after following a disciplinary process. With an employee in jail that presents obvious practical difficulties, so the process should be in writing.

In conclusion, unless the employee is convicted and handed a lengthy prison sentence, you would be well advised not to dismiss him because of his offence. Even if he is handed a prison sentence, you will be required to consider whether or not it would be possible to hold this employee's job open for him pending his return. However, you may want to consider disciplining this employee through the company's disciplinary procedure so that there is some record of this incident on his file.

The answer may be slightly different if the company has a contractual right to dismiss the employee for conduct which may 'bring the company into disrepute'. Whether or not the employee's actions in this case are capable of bringing the company into disrepute is a question of fact which may be affected by the seniority of the employee. For example, if it is the MD brawling on the aircraft, then his name will be inextricably linked with the company's name, whereas if it is a very junior employee then the company's name may never be mentioned in connection with the matter. However, even if there is a contractual power to dismiss here, the dismissal can still be unreasonable under the law of unfair dismissal.

Question

There is a direct conflict of evidence between two employees involved in a disciplinary. We don't know who to believe. What should we do?

Solution

In these circumstances the first thing that an employer should do is to carry out further investigation to establish whether one or other of the employees' evidence can be corroborated. This may mean obtaining further witness statements or alternatively obtaining collecting other forms of evidence, such as CCTV evidence or other forms of physical evidence.

In order to take disciplinary action against one or other of the employees you should be satisfied that you have a genuine belief that the employee committed the alleged act or omission founded upon a reasonable investigation. Ultimately if you do not have enough evidence to establish a genuine belief that one of the employees has committed an act of misconduct then you may be advised to drop disciplinary proceedings altogether.

Alternatively, you can exercise your judgement to believe one employee and not the other. This is legitimate, as long as you have a rational basis for believing one and not the other.

Question

We are carrying out an investigation into the theft of items by a member of staff. He has been suspended and denies the allegations. We have been told that we have to carry out a "reasonable" investigation. How far do we have to go for the investigation to be reasonable?

Solution

First of all, with regard to the extent of a 'reasonable' investigation into an allegation of misconduct, this will vary from case to case and will depend on the particular circumstances. In cases where there is an allegation of theft, the extent of the investigation will vary depending on whether the employee has been 'caught red handed' or whether there is mere suspicion. The employer will undoubtedly need to carry out a more thorough investigation in the latter case. Where the employee admits the misconduct further investigation is not usually necessary, even when the employee admits the misconduct in a rather round about manner. For example, in the case of Integrated Care Ltd v Smith the Scottish Employment Appeal Tribunal held that no further investigation was required when an employee stated 'I'm not saying I didn't say it' in response to allegations that she had been verbally abusive to a patient.

The investigation carried out should also be proportionate to the seriousness of the allegation against the employee – usually the more serious the allegation and the possible outcome, the more thorough the investigation should be. As theft is undoubtedly a serious allegation it will usually therefore require a more thorough investigation. In addition, the size of the employer and the extent of its resources will have a bearing upon how far an employer should go in investigating the allegation.

In terms of the means of investigation, often the most important component of a 'reasonable investigation' is the taking of corroborative witness statements. As this case involves theft the evidence of others who witnessed the employee thieving or handling the stolen items, or who were working in the vicinity where the thefts took place, or who were working with the employee at the time the thefts took place, or even heard him bragging about the thefts will be important. Employers do not need to necessarily go so far as interviewing every possible witness once a fact is established, but an investigation may be flawed if, for example, you rely on statements from employees giving second hand accounts when you could have got a first hand account from another witness but failed to do so.

Consideration also needs to be given as to whether any physical evidence is required. In a case involving allegations of theft, physical evidence may include CCTV evidence. We do not believe that it will it be necessary for employers to go to the extent of obtaining forensic evidence such as finger printing, but if this does settle the matter then this may be an option the employer may want to consider if an employer has the means to obtain such evidence.

Further, if the police also conduct an investigation the employer is also entitled to use the police investigations as part of its investigations, although usually it is advisable for the employer to carry out its own investigations and not just rely solely on the police report.

Question

We have been investigating an allegation of bullying by a manager, Bruce, and several witnesses have come forward to say that they have witnessed the bullying, but they are very reluctant to put their name to a witness statement. They say they feel very awkward and vulnerable if they do so. How do we handle this?

Solution

The reluctant witness is a problem commonly encountered by employers.

The first step here would be to try to encourage the employees to agree to put their evidence into statements with their names. In order to take any action against Bruce, he will be entitled to know the case against him. In this case, as the allegations against Bruce relate to bullying, the only way that Bruce will be able to defend himself against the claims is by knowing whom he has allegedly bullied. Consequently, if witness statements do not divulge these details, it may be difficult to justify taking disciplinary action against Bruce.

You should try to establish from speaking to the employees why they are unwilling to sign the statements. If it is because they fear retaliation from Bruce you could re-assure them by explaining that they will be protected from any bullying or harassment by Bruce as a result of them giving witness evidence against Bruce even if nothing comes of the allegations. You can tell them that any retaliation by Bruce will result in serious disciplinary action against him. There is also a "safety in numbers" point. If several witnesses came forward, each can feel more secure.

You can also appeal to employees' duties toward the employer and their colleagues. If Bruce is a bully, he must be stopped, and they have a responsibility to help you achieve that.

In the event that the employees are still reluctant to put their names to a witness statement you can ask them to provide a version of events in an anonymous witness statement. If this is going to be done you should follow the guidelines given in the case of Linfood Cash and Carry v Thomson 1989, in particular, the employees should give their evidence in a written statement (although subsequently sections can be redacted in order to preserve anonymity), corroborative evidence should be obtained (for example, you should check whether the evidence can be corroborated by witness evidence from witnesses who will put their name to their statement rather than by other anonymous statements) and checks should be carried out to find out whether the employee giving the anonymous statement has a grudge against Bruce. You need to satisfy yourself that evidence has not been fabricated or embellished.

Question

How do I effectively deal with excessive personal phone and text usage in the workplace?

Solution

We advise employers to put in place a policy setting out expected parameters for personal phone and text usage in the workplace. The policy could state that employees should switch personal mobile phones off during working hours and only make personal calls or send personal text messages during breaks. It could also state that you should not encourage personal calls during working hours and should ask friends and family to contact you outside of working hours except in cases of genuine urgency. If you do put in place such a policy it must also make it clear that disciplinary action may follow in the event that an employee breaches your policy on acceptable personal phone usage during working hours so that you can take disciplinary action in the event of excessive use of personal mobiles.

It is important to ensure that your policy reflects what actually happens in your workplace, therefore if you do allow employees to use their mobile phones but require them to keep them on silent mode during the working day make this clear in your policy.

Undoubtedly, monitoring personal phone usage can be difficult, and even more so in the case of text messaging which can be easily concealed; however, hopefully by putting in place and circulating a policy setting out what is expected of employees they will be deterred from using their personal phones to excess whilst at work. In the event that you do find that an employee has been making excessive calls or sending excessive messages on his mobile phone then you should then take disciplinary action in accordance with your policy.

With regards to company mobile phones excessive personal phone calls and text messages can be monitored far more easily by analysing the bill each month. Again you should ideally put in place a policy setting out the extent that employees in possession of a company mobile are permitted to use the phone for personal calls and messages. You could make it clear in such a policy that employees will have to forfeit the company mobile in the event that they make excessive personal calls and text messages and that disciplinary action may also be taken.

Question

Next week we will be seeing two brothers (independently of one another) for a formal disciplinary to answer a number of very serious allegations with regards to suspected fraud. If guilty, this will almost certainly lead to their dismissal. The concern we have is that one (or both) may request that their brother acts as their companion.

As both are subject to disciplinary procedures, can we prohibit this?

Solution

Yes. The right to be accompanied only applies where a worker makes a "reasonable request" to be accompanied. The ACAS Code on Disciplinary Procedures recognises that it would not be reasonable for a worker to request the presence of someone who would prejudice the hearing. In this case, if the brothers do request each other, you could simply tell them that – while they do have the right to be accompanied – they will need to request someone else.

Question

Dave suffered an accident at work. Since then, he has made frequent comments about "taking the company to the cleaners". Last month, Dave went off sick. His medical certificates have all read: "Bad back due to accident at work". Last week, you got a medical report from Dave's medical specialist, which, in broad terms, read: "Dave can't walk further than 100m without sitting down and can't sit down for long periods. I cannot be certain at this stage whether the condition has been caused by the accident at work – more tests will be needed – but it is highly unlikely Dave will be able to return to his old role for the foreseeable future. He may be able to undertake light duties in future but not for at least six months after he has received specialist treatment".

Dave's suspicious managers had Dave followed. Over the course of two days, a private investigator filmed Dave walking quite comfortably round the corner to buy a newspaper and sitting for half an hour in his local pub. The managers want to dismiss Dave on the grounds of dishonesty.

What do you do?

Solution

It is doubtless tempting in this situation to dismiss Dave for dishonesty. And, in reality, Dave probably has been exaggerating his condition and is now enjoying his time off.

However, you have only seen him walking "round the corner" and sitting for "half an hour". On close examination, this is not really inconsistent with the medical evidence. A dismissal on the grounds of gross misconduct is unlikely to be fair.

On the other hand, if you take the medical evidence at face value, you might have good reasons for terminating Dave's employment on the grounds of medical capability. You have been told it is highly unlikely he will be able to return to his old role. You could carry out a cost/benefit analysis now and decide what – if any – role Dave is likely to be able to perform in six months' time. Alternatively, it might be safer to wait for Dave to receive his specialist treatment in six months time and assess the

Harry Sherrard

situation then. You will have to consider what – if anything – Dave's specialist says he is able to do and what – if any – roles you have which Dave could conceivably do. A dismissal on medical grounds has a much better prospect of being deemed fair than a dismissal on conduct grounds. Certainly, you should involve your employer's liability insurers at an early stage since – as the accident took place at work – they are likely to foot the bill if his employment is terminated on the grounds of ill health.

Question

You have just concluded a grievance appeal meeting with Maureen. Maureen is always complaining about something – her personnel file has a drawer to itself - and this grievance has been particularly gruelling as Maureen dug up several alleged instances of "blatant sex discrimination" going back the past five years. No sooner is the meeting over than Maureen sends you an e-mail saying: "I feel the way you disregarded all the points I raised in my grievance appeal meeting was a blatant act of sex discrimination!"

What should you do?

Solution

In the case of Petherbridge v Mudchute Association (2005), the EAT held that a grievance about the manner in which a grievance was held could in itself amount to a grievance.

Therefore, irritating though it may be, the only sensible course of action here is to organise yet another meeting to discuss Maureen's latest grievance (see page 81).

Question

An employee has resigned, raising a litany of complaints about her treatment. In the absence of the statutory grievance procedures, how do we deal with this?

Solution

Under the statutory grievance procedures, it became common for employees to send long grievance letters after they had resigned from their employment. The reasons for this is because under the old statutory procedures employees could be prevented from bringing certain claims (discrimination and constructive unfair dismissal claims) before tribunal if they had not previously brought the matter to the attention of the employer under the grievance procedure. If the employer then failed to deal with the grievance and the employee subsequently brought a successful unfair dismissal or discrimination claim, the tribunal could uplift his compensation by up to 50%. Consequently, employers were required to follow the grievance procedure on receipt of such a letter or rant!

Now that we no longer have the statutory grievance procedures, employees are no longer prevented from bringing claims including discrimination and constructive unfair dismissal claims if they do not first raise a grievance with their employer. Employers no longer run the risk of compensation being automatically uplifted by up to 50% if they just ignore the letter. Consequently, you can simply send a quick note thanking her for her letter and leave it there. However, there still may be good reasons to meet with the employee to discuss her complaints. The greatest incentive for doing this is that by meeting with the employee you may be able to resolve her complaints and thus avoid a tribunal claim. If the complaints are not well founded, you will have the opportunity to put across the other side of the story which may even deter her from bringing a tribunal claim, if she was considering doing so. Alternatively, if her complaints cannot be resolved and she does bring a tribunal claim, you will at least have a heads up on the type of case you will have to defend.

Question

What can we do to prevent an employee making excessive invalid grievances, often upsetting colleagues in the process?

Solution

Whilst it is tempting to ignore grievances from the serial grievant generally we would not advise you to do this because, no matter how trivial you consider a grievance to be, the matter raised may be very important to the employee and by going through the grievance procedure hopefully you can resolve the issue and bring an end to the matter.

The employee's only redress here is to resign and claim constructive dismissal. Whilst under the ACAS Code the consequences of failing to comply with a grievance procedure upon receipt of a grievance are not as draconian as under the old (and now repealed) statutory procedures, failure to deal with an employee's grievance could still entitle the employee to resign and bring a constructive unfair dismissal claim. This is based on breach of the implied term that an employer will 'reasonably and promptly afford a reasonable opportunity to its employees to obtain redress of any grievance" (W A Goold (Pearmark) Ltd v McConnell & anor 1995) or alternatively based on breach of the implied term of mutual trust and confidence.

You may be able to defend such a claim if you can show that the grievances were not reasonable, and as a result the implied duties described above were not fundamentally breached by the employer, so as to entitle the employee to resign and bring a constructive unfair dismissal claim. Alternatively, if an employee brings a constructive unfair dismissal claim based on breach of the implied term of mutual trust and confidence you could attempt to defeat the claim by asserting that the Claimant's conduct in raising excessive and invalid grievances meant that he or she (rather than the employer) had breached the implied duty of trust and confidence in the first instance. This may bar the employee from relying on the employer's subsequent breach of the mutual duty of trust and confidence, although whether this argument will succeed is currently a contested issue.

If the employee does ultimately succeed at tribunal remember tribunals have the discretion to uplift any award for compensation by up to 25% where they find that an employer has failed to comply with the ACAS

Code of Practice on disciplinary and grievance procedures. Therefore the safer option is usually to follow some kind of grievance procedure.

That said, however, there are steps that you can take to discourage employees from raising excessive grievances. First of all you could make it clear in your policies that employees must not abuse the grievance procedure by raising excessive and invalid grievances. You could also make it clear in your policies that you will not re-consider grievances which have already been dealt with unless there is a substantial and significant change in the circumstances. It is also important that you make sure that your grievance procedure is non-contractual to give you flexibility to depart from it which may be useful if you find that you have a serial grievant, in which case you may decide to depart from your full procedure by responding in writing to the grievance rather than holding a meeting with the employee.

In extreme circumstances only would you consider taking disciplinary action against a serial grievant as it is very rarely going to be the case that you can show that the employee's actions in raising excessive and invalid grievances amount to an act of misconduct. If as a result of the employee's excessive and invalid grievances the relationship between that employee and his colleagues breaks down disciplinary action may be appropriate. The safer option, however, is usually to deal with the grievance, even if only by following an abbreviated version of your grievance procedure.

DISCRIMINATION ON GROUNDS OF RACE AND RELIGION

Question

We have a mixed race workforce. Can we insist on English being spoken in the workplace, as English speaking employees have complained of exclusion?

Solution

It is potentially indirect race discrimination to prevent employees from speaking their own native language in the workplace. The discrimination is indirect because there is a condition or requirement being imposed on the whole workforce i.e. a requirement to speak English. This adversely affects non-native English speakers and is therefore potentially indirect race discrimination with regard to those employees. However, indirect discrimination may be justified. Here the employer's justification would be that English speaking employees have complained of exclusion and that, in the overall interests of the better and efficient functioning of the business, English should be spoken.

However, that justification argument would probably only apply if the requirement was limited to conversations involving work. An employer is unlikely to be able to justify a rule requiring foreign employees to speak to each other in English during their coffee breaks or lunch breaks. In order to justify indirect discrimination, an employer must show it has a legitimate business aim and that the means it is using to achieve that aim are proportionate. Not wanting employees to feel "excluded" may be a legitimate aim but is a requirement that all employees speak English all the time – even in their own time - a proportionate means of achieving that aim? The fact that English people might feel "excluded" because they can't understand every conversation they overhear is unlikely to be enough. Why, for example, are we not requiring English speaking employees to speak slowly and clearly to each other in their lunch breaks so that foreign employees can understand them and not feel "excluded"? Should we ban the use of colloquial terms that foreigners might find it hard to understand? Are we going to prevent groups of employees from speaking quietly to each other for fear that those out of earshot may feel excluded? If we are going to argue that it is "proportionate" to require all employees to speak English all of the time, we must expect arguments that it would also be "proportionate" to take further steps to ensure that all employees can understand each others' conversations and that could lead to ridiculous and unnecessary rules.

If you do impose a rule that English must be spoken in the workplace (with the exception of lunch breaks and other breaks when other languages can be used) then hopefully that will be enough to make the English-speakers feel that you have done something to deal with their feelings of exclusion.

Question

We have a strict uniform policy. We received an application from a female Muslim who wears a hijab. Our uniform makes no allowance for this.

How do we handle this?

Solution

The issue that could arise here is one of indirect discrimination. A ban on headscarves could in practice discriminate indirectly against a group defined with reference to race or religion. The crucial issue here is likely to be justification. Indirect discrimination can be permissible if the "rule" is held to be a proportionate means of meeting a legitimate business objective.

There can be all sorts of legitimate business objectives relating to what employees wear. One example is safety, but this seems unlikely to be relevant here. Others are concerned with the employer's "image", as presented by its employees to its customers. Within that, there can be rules that simply require, for example, a tidy appearance or, at the other end of the scale, there can be detailed uniform requirements.

On these facts, the legitimate business objective likely to apply is the presentation of an appropriate corporate image. The precise details of the uniform policy are (some of) the means by which the employer seeks to achieve that objective.

The issue is whether, given the extent of the discriminatory effect, it would be reasonably possible to preserve "an appropriate corporate image" whilst allowing headscarves to be worn. It could be rather difficult to persuade a tribunal that this would not be reasonably possible. There are various ways that the policy could be adapted in the circumstances. For example, appropriately coloured or shaped headscarves could be supplied to those wishing to wear them. The additional cost in supplying these would only be minimal and in fact, there might even be savings with respect to any alternative headgear for which the uniform policy normally provides. Therefore, any arguments on cost would not weigh heavily in the "proportionate" balance.

One point to note here is that there are specific legislative provisions and case law showing that "exceptions" to uniform policies are expected to be made to allow Sikhs to wear their turbans. Similar reasoning is likely to be applied in the case of headscarves worn for race or religious reasons.

Unless you can produce some compelling reason why the uniform policy cannot, whilst preserving an appropriate corporate image, be changed to allow the wearing of headscarves, to reject an applicant because she wishes, on race or religious grounds, to cover her head might well open you to a successful discrimination claim. It would be a much safer option to adapt the existing uniform policy to allow for headscarves to be worn.

Question

We have learned that an employee is a member of the BNP and other employees object. How do I handle this?

Solution

If continuing to employ this particular employee is going to cause discontent amongst your other employees you may consider dismissing him.

Generally, tribunals frown upon dismissals of employees for something that they do outside of work. This can be seen where an employee commits a criminal offence outside of work. However, you may be able to rely on the fair reason of 'some other substantial reason' on the basis that the employee's colleagues are unhappy about continuing to work with this employee. Strong objections will need to be raised in order to ensure such a dismissal is deemed fair, and you as the employer would need to show that you have taken all reasonable steps to overcome the other employee's objections. Alternatively, if it is clear in your disciplinary policies that an employee can be dismissed for acts committed outside of work which make a colleague unacceptable to other colleagues, you may also be able to rely on misconduct as a reason to dismiss this employee.

If you dismiss him or take other disciplinary action against him due to him being a member of the BNP could this employee bring a direct discrimination claim against you based on the protected characteristic of religion or belief?

Under the Equality Act a 'belief' is defined as 'any religious or philosophical belief and a reference to belief includes a reference to a lack of belief'. This definition is not very comprehensive but there have been a number of cases that have sought to further define what will suffice as a 'belief' (although these cases were decided before the Equality Act came into force they should still be relevant).

One recent case in particular has suggested that belief in a political party can be capable of amounting to a belief protected against unlawful discrimination (Grainger plc and others v Nicholson 2010 – Employment Appeal Tribunal); however the same case held that for such a belief to be protected it must be 'worthy of respect in a democratic society, not be incompatible with human dignity and not conflict with the fundamental rights of others'. Consequently, belief in the BNP could on this basis be deemed incapable of constituting a belief.

In addition, prior to the Nicholson case there were two tribunal cases brought by BNP members claiming discrimination, both of which were unsuccessful - Baggs v Fudge 2005 and Finnon v Asda 2005. The facts of the Finnon v Asda case are similar to this scenario; the employee Mr Finnon was dismissed as a result of his involvement in BNP activities outside of work which were published, and which his colleagues, customers and the local community found unacceptable. In this case the tribunal dismissed his claim on the grounds that they did not find that British Nationalism or the British National Party had a clear belief system or a profound belief affecting the way of life or view of the world.

In summary, therefore, taking disciplinary action against this employee on account of his BNP membership is unlikely to amount to discrimination because of the protected characteristic of religion or belief. In fact, BNP members are already barred from some organisations and cannot work as police or prison officers, and most recently the education secretary, Michael Gove, has pledged to bar BNP members from working as teachers.

CONTRACTS OF EMPLOYMENT

Question

An employee comes to work exhausted because he has a part time evening job. Can we stop him doing this, and do the Working Time Regulations assist?

Solution

The first thing to do is to check the contract of employment. Ideally there should be a clause prohibiting secondary employment, which would mean that the employee is in breach of contract and disciplinary sanctions could be applied. In the absence of such a clause we turn to the Working Time Regulations ('WTR'), which contain a 48-hour limit on average weekly working time and entitle workers to a daily rest period of not less than 11 consecutive hours. Taking each of these provisions in turn:

The WTR do not address the situation in which a worker works for more than one employer. However, it is likely that an employee with more than one job should not work for more than 48 hours in total. Employers are required to take all 'reasonable steps' to ensure that the 48-hour limit is complied with. The precise nature of 'reasonable steps' will vary between employers depending on circumstances. In this case, the employer knows that the employee has a part time evening job and has reason for suspecting that he may be exceeding the 48-hour average weekly limit. The employer should remind the employee that he should not work more than 48 hours per week.

Under the WTR workers are entitled to a daily rest period of not less than 11 consecutive hours. However, this is only an entitlement, which means that workers can voluntarily forgo their rest breaks if they choose to do so, and employers are only required to make sure that their workers can take their rest.

Unfortunately, this means that the WTR themselves do not provide an answer. However, if the employee's performance is seriously affected by his exhaustion then this could potentially lead to a dismissal for incapability, which is one of the six potentially fair reasons for dismissal. The best approach therefore would be to "warn" (or at least "counsel") the employee that by exhausting himself in his other job he is jeopardising his employment with you because of poor performance.

Of course, it would be easier if there were a clear contractual provision about not having secondary employment, but the absence of a clear contractual provision does not mean that the employer is not entitled to act against any performance consequences of secondary employment.

The usual rules would apply – the employer would need to go through some sort of performance assessment and warning process before the ultimate sanction of dismissal could be applied. The issue here is performance and the problem has to be tackled as such.

Question

Pluto Communications has a 9 to 5 receptionist's role, currently split between Marjorie, who works 9 to 1.30, and Denise, who works 1.30 to 5. Denise has gone on maternity leave and Anita has been recruited on a fixed term nine month contract to cover Denise's position.

Pluto is a company that provides staff with a number of benefits. Anita has questioned how her salary and benefits have been calculated, and seems to be suggesting that she is missing out on benefits received by other members of staff.

How do you approach this problem, and what rules do you consider?

Would your answer be different if there were two full time equivalent receptionist positions, with the other position held by a single fulltime permanent member of staff?

Solution

You need to consider the Part Time Workers (Prevention of less Favourable Treatment) Regulations 2000 and Fixed Term Employee (Prevention of Less Favourable Treatment) Regulations 2002.

Anita is both a part time and a fixed term employee, and therefore both sets of Regulations potentially apply to her.

Under the Part Time Workers Regulations, Anita is entitled to a strict pro-rata of all benefits, provided she is able to compare herself to a full time employee undertaking similar work. In this case, the only other receptionist is another part time employee, and therefore she has no full time comparator. Consequently she is not able to progress a claim under the Part Time Workers Regulations.

Under the Fixed Term Employee Regulations employees employed on a fixed term, often called 'temps', are entitled to the same benefits as permanent members of staff. However, the rules are less strict than those under the Part Time Workers Regulations, and the employer can adopt the package approach. This means that an employer can pay a slightly higher hourly rate to compensate for any benefits that are not given.

For the Fixed Term Employee Regulations to apply there must be a comparable permanent employee (similar to the Part Time Worker Regulations, as set out above). Here, Marjorie is a permanent employee, so Anita has her comparator, and is able to bring a claim under the Fixed Term Employee Regulations.

The answer would be different if there was a full time permanent receptionist, because, under the Part Time Workers Regulations, Anita would have her full time comparator and needs to be provided the pro-rata benefits that are being provided to the full timer.

Although it is unavoidable that Anita will be part time and therefore potentially subject to the Part Time Worker Regulations, it is possible to avoid the Fixed Term Employee Regulations completely, by not employing her as a fixed term employee at all. She could be engaged on a normal rolling contract, and as long as she is dismissed within 12 months, she cannot claim unfair dismissal. If it turns out that she goes over the 12 months, she can be fairly dismissed for "some other substantial reason" namely to make way for the return of the maternity absentee.

Question

We have made an offer of employment to a senior employee, who has resigned from his existing position to take up our offer. He has to relocate and has exchanged contracts on the sale of his house. Due to the sudden and unexpected loss of a major customer, we no longer have this vacancy and want to withdraw the offer. What are the implications?

Solution

The offer of employment has been made and the employee has accepted this, so a binding contract has been created. The employee is therefore entitled to be paid his notice period. In many contracts there will be a probationary period at the beginning during which the notice period is just 1 week. However, if this was a senior employee, that may not have been the case, so whatever contractual notice period was in the contract needs to be honoured.

Although the situation is highly unfortunate, it is unlikely that the employee will be able to bring any other claims against the prospective employer. It is conceivable that a claim in negligence could be brought in these circumstances if the employer had withdrawn the offer for no apparent reason. Even in extreme circumstances that would be difficult for an employee to prove, and in this instance the employer had justification in that there was the unexpected loss of a major customer.

Of course, the employer can always make an ex-gratia payment in these circumstances.

Question

An employee with a six month notice period has resigned, to go to another job. I don't want to pay the six months' notice. Is there any way around this?

Solution

One way round this is to agree with the employee a shorter period of notice. If the employee can start his new job at an earlier date he may be keen to agree this. This would be a mutual variation of contract. By agreeing a shorter notice period with the employee the employee will remain bound by any post termination restrictions in his contract of employment, for example, clauses preventing him working for a competitor or soliciting your clients.

In the event that the employee does not agree to a shorter notice period, we would not advise you to impose a shorter notice period on this employee. This is because by doing so not only could the employee bring a claim against you for the remainder of his notice period, he could also bring an unfair dismissal claim against you on the basis that by refusing to let him work his notice period you have effectively turned his resignation into a dismissal.

Whilst any award is likely to be fairly small as the employee has found a new job, meaning he is not likely to receive any compensation under the compensatory award for loss of earnings, he would receive the basic award - one week's pay (capped at £400 per week) for each year of employment (up to a maximum of 20 weeks).

Further, as you would have breached the employee's contract, the rest of his contract would fall away meaning that he will no longer be bound by any restrictive covenants.

Question

One of our Directors was given a new contract of employment two years ago, with restrictive covenants. He did not sign it, but has worked under it since then. He is now leaving and claims that the restrictive covenants do not apply as he did not sign the contract.

Is he correct?

Solution

The Director is probably correct.

Employers often believe that they can rely on the "if you do not object then you have accepted the contract" principle, but this is an unreliable approach.

Cases show that contractual clauses which have immediate impact on the employee can indeed be deemed to have been accepted by performance of the contract. Thus, terms relating to hours, place of work, content of job, payment rates etc. all do have immediate impact, and once the employee has worked the hours under the contract and accepts payment at the due rate, he is likely to be deemed by virtue of this past performance to have accepted the contract.

However, courts have drawn a distinction between these kinds of terms and other terms which have no immediate impact on the employee. This will include such things as mobility clauses and restrictive covenants. Unless and until the employer seeks to enforce those clauses, they have no effect on the employee and he is therefore not bound by them.

In the case of Aparau v Iceland Frozen Foods, the employee had not agreed to a mobility clause, even though she had continued to work for the employer without objection for over a year after a contract containing the mobility clause was issued to her. This was on the basis that the mobility clause did not have an immediate practical effect. Unless an employer can establish conclusively that a change has already had an effect on the employee, and the employee continued to work without objection after that point, it will be difficult to argue that an employee has by their actions impliedly agreed to a change.

In this case, the contractual confidentiality and restrictive covenants will almost certainly therefore not apply, although there are common law duties of confidentiality upon which the employer can rely. Clearly, it is much more satisfactory to ensure that senior employees are bound by the provisions in their contract.

The moral is always to ensure that contracts are signed. In an extreme case, it is possible to threaten termination of employment if contracts are not signed and returned.

Question

George has been off sick for about nine months. A recent specialist's report has indicated that he is very unlikely to be able to return to work for the foreseeable future. George is aged 55 and is entitled to ill health early retirement under his employer's pension scheme. His contract of employment states that he has to give four weeks' notice of resignation, and the employer has to give him twelve weeks' notice of termination.

If George takes the option of ill health early retirement, how would you characterise the termination of his employment and, what entitlement does he have to notice?

Solution

There are three ways in which an employment contract can come to an end. Dismissal, resignation, or the less common termination by mutual consent.

If George resigns, he would have to give four weeks' notice and the employer could, in theory, ask him to "work out" his notice. In practice of course, that is meaningless in that he is off sick and not in receipt of any pay. By resigning, George could jeopardise the ill health retirement benefits, so he is unlikely to do this.

If the employer decides to dismiss him then the 12 week notice period will apply. Note that in these situations, even though George is now on zero pay, the termination of the contract requires payment at his full normal contractual rate (section 87 of the Employment Rights Act 1996). In addition, the employer needs to remember that fair dismissal procedures apply and a dismissal process involving a meeting with him and the right to appeal would need to be followed. Furthermore, although this does seem like a reasonably clear-cut capability dismissal, there is still the risk of an unfair dismissal claim.

On balance therefore the best way of dealing with this is to handle it as a termination by mutual consent. Each party in effect waives the notice period provisions, and the employee simply goes directly from employment to ill health early retirement. This of course will need to be agreed with the pension providers, who will need both medical evidence to support his application and will also need to be advised by the employer that termination of the employment was as a result of the ill health.

Question

Your business is in a state of flux. Longer term it seems clear that staffing at the present levels will be adequate. But for the immediate future there is a need for more staff. What is not clear is for how long the additional staff will be needed. It is unlikely to be for less than 9 months: it may turn out to be for as much as 18 months. Should appointments made now be on fixed term contracts, or temporary contracts, or what?

Solution

The law does not (except in special cases, for example covering for maternity leave, which are not relevant here) expressly recognise "temporary" contracts. It does recognise fixed term (or "limited term" contracts) but with a much more limited effect than is often thought. In particular, the expiry of a fixed term contract without renewal is a "dismissal" for unfair dismissal purposes. And, whilst "expiry of a fixed term contract" can be "some other substantial reason" for dismissal, this does not guarantee that such "dismissal" (in fact non-renewal) will be accepted by a tribunal as "reasonable".

When a contract of employment ends – whether it is called "temporary" or "permanent" or "fixed term" or whatever – the law asks "does the way in which it ended qualify as 'dismissal'?" And if it was the employer that ended it (or a fixed term expired without renewal) the answer to that question is "yes".

"Dismissal", of itself, does not give the dismissed employee any right to any remedy against the dismissing employer. For there to be any such right, the dismissal has to be "unfair", or it has to involve some other illegality such as discrimination on forbidden grounds – race, sex, etc. In those latter cases, even though the discriminatory act may involve dismissal, the employee can act in relation to the discrimination, which means s/he does not have to have any qualifying service. But where there is no discriminatory element the employee needs 12 months' service before s/he can claim unfair dismissal.

So, in the first instance anyway, the crucial question when an employee is "dismissed" (including by expiry of a fixed term contract) is not whether the contract was called "temporary" or "permanent" or "fixed term" or whatever but whether s/he had, at the date of "dismissal", been employed for less than 12 months. If that is the case s/he cannot claim unfair dismissal: absent any alleged discrimination, the employer cannot be called upon to justify the dismissal. If that is not the case then, even if the contract was called "temporary" or "fixed term" or some variation on those themes, the employee has the right to claim unfair dismissal: the employer might have to justify the "dismissal".

What all this means is that, just from the perspective of protecting yourself against unfair dismissal claims, labelling contracts of those you now take on as "temporary" or "fixed term" might be regarded as superfluous. If the contracts (however they are labelled) in fact last for less than 12 months, then you do not need the labels. Even a "permanent" employee with less than 12 months' service cannot claim unfair dismissal. If in fact they last for 12 months or more, then no label will preclude the possibility of an unfair dismissal claim.

That any such labelling might be "superfluous" in the sense just described does not, however, mean that you should just keep quiet. In an HR sense, if you are making an appointment that you genuinely expect may not turn out to be permanent it would be "good practice" to say so. From a legal point of view, if the judgment on whether a dismissal was "fair" or "unfair" does fall to be made it has to be made with reference to "reasonableness" and the dismissal of an employee who has been "warned", on appointment, that the job may not last beyond a certain date will be more "reasonable" than one where the employee had not been so "warned". But, and this is the real point, although a "temporary" or "fixed term" label may contribute to a finding of "fair" dismissal, it will not guarantee it. The only "guarantee" (and this only to the extent of making sure that any cases that are brought will be lost – there is no way of ensuring that no cases are brought) would be to terminate the contracts concerned before the 12 months' service had been accumulated. Given that you may need the additional staff for as much as 18 months, that is probably not an attractive approach.

The event for which you wish to cater is, simply, that (possibly in more than 12 months time) you need to terminate contracts because you have too many employees. In other words what is in prospect here is, just, "redundancy". If there are other reasons for terminating employees – e.g. misconduct or incapability – then you will be able to do that anyway (even if the employee concerned has built up 12 months' service) using "normal" procedures. "Redundancy" is expressly statutorily specified as a "fair" reason for dismissal and an important element in the fairness of the dismissal is "selection".

You could cover that point by making it clear to those whom you are now appointing that, in the event of any future redundancy, the selection method used will hit them before it hits any existing employee. In the circumstances in which you currently find yourself, the adoption of such a selection method is unlikely to be characterised as either "outside the range of reasonable responses" in the context of unfair dismissal law or not "objectively justifiable" in the context of discrimination law. And provided the appointee had been made clearly aware of it at the time of appointment it is unlikely that s/he could then argue that it was "unreasonable" from a personal perspective.

If you want to reinforce that message by, additionally, labelling the contract in some specific way, then there is no overriding legal reason why you should not do so. But, if you wish to do that, a "temporary" label might be better than "fixed term". There are two reasons for this.

First, as you do not know the length of time for which you will need current appointees – "it is unlikely to be for less than 9 months: it may turn out to be for as much as 18 months" – there may be difficulties in defining what the "fixed" term is. That has to be specified – by date or with reference to the occurrence or non-occurrence of some external event – when the appointment is made.

Secondly, "fixed term" employees are – but "temporary" employees are not – covered by the Fixed Term Employees (Prevention of Less Favourable Treatment) Regulations 2002. This means that fixed term employees must receive a package of pay and benefits that is commensurate with permanent staff.

BUSINESS TRANSFERS

Question

We have lost a contract to one of our competitors and are convinced that TUPE applies, but the other company is refusing to accept this.

What do we do with our employees?

Solution

In this situation the employer is faced with something of a Hobson's choice.

If you are correct in your belief that TUPE applies, your staff should be employed by the other company once the transfer has taken place. You can, therefore, tell the employees that their employment with you is ended, and that they should present themselves for work at 9 am on the Monday morning on the doorstep of the transferee. Clearly that is an uncomfortable situation for the employer, but precisely this has occurred in a number of situations that we know about. If the transferee persists in not employing the staff, this would be a dismissal, and, since the dismissal is for a TUPE related reason, the dismissal would be automatically unfair.

The alternative for the transferor is to make the staff redundant, paying them the appropriate level of statutory and (if applicable) contractual redundancy pay. To a large extent this is a contradictory approach by the employer, since if he is correct that TUPE applies, the employees are not redundant. Plus, the transferor is paying redundancy costs when in fact he should not have incurred that expense. Nonetheless this is in some respects a better way of dealing with staff as the outcome described above is unattractive.

Unless the transferor asks the employees to sign a compromise agreement in return for payment of the redundancy pay, both the transferor and transferee are open to tribunal proceedings by the affected staff. It is usual in a TUPE situation that the employee would join both the transferor and transferee as respondents, to hedge his bets. If it is a TUPE transfer (which can only be determined in the fullness of time by a tribunal) then liability for the unfair dismissal passes to the transferee. If, however, the transferor was wrong all along and it was not a TUPE transfer, liability would stay with him. If the transferor has taken the second of the two options above, and has paid redundancy, he is probably going to be alright, because in the scenario that it turns out not to have been a TUPE transfer, the employees were indeed redundant and the employer has therefore acted correctly.

It is worth repeating that there is no short-term method for the parties to determine whether or not a TUPE transfer has indeed or is about to take place. That can only be determined by a tribunal which needs to be brought by one or more of the affected employees.

TUPE consultation with affected staff needs to take place in advance of the TUPE transfer. A protective award of 13 weeks' pay per employee may be made if there is a failure to consult. Clearly in this scenario the transferor has, presumably, done his best to consult, but in the absence of any information from the transferee about proposed measures it is difficult for transferor to consult effectively. There is potentially joint and several liability as between transferor and transferee for the protective award if there is a failure to consult, although the tribunal could make an award just against the transferee if it thinks that the transferee was wholly to blame for the lack of consultation.

Question

Your company has taken over a contract to supply cleaning services to a number of offices across the region. You are due to take over the contracts in three weeks' time. Last month, you started a series of road-shows around the various offices telling the cleaners in those offices that you were taking over the contracts and that they would be transferring to you under TUPE. You offered the cleaners the opportunity to elect representatives for the purposes of TUPE consultation but they declined. You have now sent out letters to the cleaners detailing their new contracts; one of the cleaners has come to you saying: "What about TUPE consultation? Aren't you going to do any?"

You are a bit flummoxed as you have spent several weeks doing just that, but the cleaner is adamant that she is going to take you to tribunal for failure to consult.

What should you do?

Solution

TUPE consultation requirements are very specific: they need to take place with employee representatives of employees who might be affected by the transfer and, importantly, both the transferor and the transferee are required to consult with their own employees. In this case, you are the transferee. However, you have consulted with the employees of the transferor. This will not satisfy the TUPE Regulations – as the transferor needs to consult with its own staff.

In this sort of situation, transferors can be unwilling to carry out any consultation themselves – they've just lost a contract and probably have better things to think about than helping you with your consultation. However, both the transferee and the transferor can be jointly and severally liable for failure to consult. The penalty for failure to consult is up to 13 weeks' pay per affected employee.

Unlike collective redundancy situations, there is no minimum duration for TUPE consultation, except that it must begin in good time since it should take place with a view to seeking agreement on any envisaged measures that the transferee intends to take following the transfer.

Here, therefore, we should place pressure on the transferor to elect representatives and inform and consult with those representatives about the proposed transfer. Our contribution will be to inform the transferor what those measures are and ensure – as far as possible – that consultation does take place. This is what should have been done in the first place.

Question

We are about to acquire some employees through a TUPE transfer. Just before the TUPE transfer took place an employee fell and injured himself in the workplace. He has not yet put in a claim, but is likely to do so after the TUPE transfer has taken place. Will this injury claim now be our responsibility?

Solution

Under TUPE all rights and liabilities relating to transferring employees transfer to the transferee. This includes liabilities under statute and tort. Consequently, liability in respect of personal injury claims will transfer– this point was made clear in the combined cases of Martin v Lancashire County Council (2) Bernadone v Pall Mall Services Group Ltd and others 2001 ('Martin' cases).

Most employers are required to have compulsory insurance to cover personal injury of their employers under the Employer's Liability (Compulsory Insurance) Act 1969. However, if an employee is injured at work before a TUPE transfer takes place and subsequently brings a personal injury claim after the transfer takes place it is unlikely that the transferee will be able to claim against its own insurance policy. This is because the employee was not the transferee's employee at the time the injury was sustained.

As a result of the Martin cases, however, cases involving a refuse collector and a catering assistant both injured at work before their employment was transferred under TUPE, the Court of Appeal held that the transferor's right of indemnity under its insurance policy in respect of the employee's personal injury claims also transferred to the transferee. On this basis therefore the employer here could claim under the transferor's insurance policy.

When transferees are inheriting employees with the potential to bring a personal injury claim it is nonetheless important that the transferee seeks appropriate indemnities from the transferor in the event that the transferor's insurers refuse to pay out, for example because of failure by the transferor to comply with the insurance policy, or in the event that the excess under the transferor's insurance policy is substantial.

Question

We engage a security company to provide security at our building, and the security company uses agency staff to fulfil the contract. We have found the service to be unsatisfactory, and we are now going to directly employ our own security staff, and end the contract with the security company. Does TUPE apply here?

Solution

The TUPE regulations do apply to situations where an employer engages a contractor to do work on its behalf but then decides to bring the work back 'in-house' – this is known as 'in-sourcing'. Consequently, TUPE can apply in this situation where a company has decided to stop using a contractor to provide security at its building and instead decided to employ security staff directly, thereby 'in-sourcing' the work.

However, only employees have rights under TUPE and as the security company here uses agency workers TUPE is unlikely to apply to them. A run of cases around 2004/2005 suggested that long term agency workers could be deemed to be employees of the end user, but more recently this trend has been reversed. The approach now is that only if it is necessary will an employment contract be implied between the agency worker and the end user. As long as there is a proper contract between the worker and the agency, and the agency continues to exercise some level of management function over the individual, it will only be in rare and exceptional cases that it will be necessary to imply a contract of employment. Therefore the likely conclusion is the security staff are agency workers, not employees, and therefore TUPE has no applicability to them. It will simply be a matter of contacting the agency and explaining that their services are no longer required. Again, as agency workers, they will not be entitled to a redundancy payment.

Question

We have taken on some employees as a result of a TUPE transfer. The manager of one of the units is a poor performer and we would like to dismiss him. His total length of service, between us and the transferor, is under 12 months. Can we just go ahead and dismiss him?

Solution

In order to bring an unfair dismissal claim an employee must have at least 12 months' continuous service in most cases, including where the employee is dismissed on capability grounds. Consequently, if you want to dismiss an employee because he is a poor performer you can do so without following a capability procedure where he has less than 12 months' continuous service, as he will not be eligible to bring an unfair dismissal claim against you.

This remains the case where an employee is dismissed following a TUPE transfer. This is because even if this manager can show that his dismissal was not because of capability reasons, but was as a result of or in connection with a TUPE transfer, which could entitle him to say that his dismissal was automatically unfair, he still must have at least one year's continuous service in order be eligible to bring such an unfair dismissal claim.

Remember, however, that employees can add on their statutory notice period of one week to their actual length of service and, as a result, if the employee has 11 months' and 3 weeks' service he can cross the 12 month qualifying hurdle and will be eligible to bring a claim.

Question

We've won a contract and will acquire employees through TUPE. We don't accept that the number of employees the transferor claims were working on the contract is accurate. How do we challenge this?

Solution

Essentially this is a factual dispute which only a tribunal can answer definitively. Under TUPE, the employment of all those 'employees employed by the transferor and assigned to the organised grouping of resources or employees that is subject to the relevant transfer' will transfer on the TUPE transfer date. But in this scenario you do not believe that the employees the transferor is saying are assigned to the contract of employment are actually working on that contract.

To deal with this pragmatically, we would suggest that in the first instance you go back to the transferor and question whether these employees are actually assigned to the grouping and seek further clarification about the roles these employees carry out. Strictly speaking under TUPE the only information a transferor has to give a transferee is the employee liability information although there is no reason why the transferor cannot at least ask further questions. You should ask to see timesheets or other documents that show employees' working hours.

If the transferor continues to insist that these employees are assigned to the contract that you are now taking over but you having carried out a thorough due diligence exercise, are convinced that they are not part of the assigned grouping of employees the position is as follows.

You can continue to refuse to take on the employees. As only the employees themselves can enforce rights under TUPE, this factual dispute will only become an issue if the employees are then dismissed by the transferor and bring unfair dismissals claims. It is important, if you decide to go down this road, that not only do you make it clear to the transferor that this is the case but also that you do not allow any of the employees concerned to start work for you.

If they do bring tribunal claims and a tribunal finds as a matter of fact that the employees were either not assigned to the grouping or only 'temporarily' assigned to the grouping, TUPE will not apply to those particular employees and you will not be liable in respect of their dismissals. On the other hand, of course, if the tribunal does find that the employees are covered by TUPE you will be liable in respect of automatic unfair dismissal claims.

Further, if TUPE does apply in this scenario, consultation with affected staff needs to take place in advance of the TUPE transfer. A protective award of 13 weeks' pay per employee may be made if there is a failure to consult. Clearly in this scenario the transferor has, presumably, done his best to consult, but in the absence of any information from the transferee about proposed measures it is difficult for transferor to consult effectively. There is potentially joint and several liability as between transferor and transferee for the protective award if there is a failure to consult, although the tribunal could make an award just against the transferee if it thinks that the transferee was wholly to blame for the lack of consultation.

There is no short-term method for the parties to determine whether or not employees are assigned to the undertaking transferred. That can only be determined by a tribunal which needs to be brought by one or more of the affected employees.

One final point that is worth mentioning is that, TUPE aside, whatever the strict legal position is as to whether these employees should transfer under TUPE, a transferor may be required to take on these employees as part of a larger commercial deal, perhaps to ensure that they secure another contract. So, employers often need to take a commercial view on whether to take on these employees irrespective of the strict position under TUPE.

Question

Your company is about to take over a business whose longer-serving employees benefit from a final salary pension scheme. As part of that scheme, senior employees who are made redundant aged 50 or over stand to get a generous lump sum payment. There is no way you can afford to match this scheme. Do you have to?

Solution

Under TUPE, employees have the right to transfer with all their terms and conditions intact when a business is transferred from one employer to another.

However, this right does not extend to occupational pension schemes (Regulation 10 of TUPE). But that does not necessarily mean you are off the hook altogether.

First of all, you will have to make available a minimum level of pension benefits to employees who were members of or eligible to join the transferor's occupational pension scheme before the transfer. You must at least provide a money purchase scheme to which you will match employee contributions up to a maximum level of 6% of the employee's gross salary.

Secondly, the definition of "occupational pension scheme" under TUPE is limited to benefits for old age, invalidity or survivor's benefit. Therefore, the exclusion does not extend to any benefits provided by a pension which do not relate to old age, invalidity or survivor's benefit. Potentially, therefore, the right of employees to receive a generous lump sum payment if they are made redundant aged 50+ will transfer to you – even though it is part of the employer's pension.

You should be especially careful if transferring in employees from the public sector – or who have previously worked for the public sector ("second generation transfers") - as there are special rules protecting their pensions and, if you transfer in employees who have previously enjoyed a public sector final salary pension, you might have to set up a pension scheme which offers them no less favourable pension benefits.

This illustrates the importance of carrying out full and proper due diligence before buying a business or even tendering for new work.

ILL HEALTH AND DISABILITY

Question

An employee gets a poor appraisal and reacts badly. The following day she calls her line manager to say she is not well enough to come to work. You later get a doctor's certificate signing her off with "work-related stress". You want to convene a follow up meeting to discuss performance issues arising from the appraisal.

Is there anything you can do?

Solution

Although it may be a route to an illness, such as depression, stress of itself is not an illness. However, it is often found on doctors' fit notes which are – at least on the face of it – evidence that an employee is unfit to attend work and eligible to receive statutory sick pay. Most sick pay policies are triggered at the same time as statutory sick pay so, if you have an occupational sick pay scheme, she will probably expect to receive payments under that scheme as well.

We recommend that employers ensure that contracts of employment allow the discretion to withhold company sick pay in these circumstances i.e. where there is a dubious "stress" note from a GP. If your contracts do not allow you this discretion then withholding sick pay would be a fundamental breach of contract entitling the employee to resign and claim constructive dismissal.

If your contracts of employment do not allow you the discretion to withhold company sick pay in these sorts of situations, you should write to the employee telling her you are going to seek further information on her medical condition from her GP and warning her that, if you are not satisfied with the response, you might claim the sick pay back later.

Either way, you are entitled to write to the employee's GP challenging or at least questioning the diagnosis.

This is not to be confused with applying for a medical report from the employee's GP, for which you will require consent under the Medical Reports Act 1998. In this process you are asking for an explanation and elaboration of the fit note, and the doctor's qualification for making the diagnosis, but you are not asking for a medical report as such.

Although it may not make you popular with the GP, you are entitled to ask questions such as:

- What expertise do you have in diagnosing mental conditions such as stress?
- What examination did you carry out in order to come to your diagnosis of 'stress'?
- Have you referred the patient to a consultant psychiatrist?

We recommend that employers have sickness polices that specifically deal with dubious "stress" fit notes. A correctly drafted policy will enable you to reserve the right to withhold company sick pay until you have had confirmation of any 'stress' diagnosis from a consultant psychiatrist. Second, you should make it clear that GP's certificates will not be considered reasonable evidence to excuse an employee from attending any disciplinary or performance hearing, and that the only evidence you would accept is a report from a consultant psychiatrist confirming that the employee is too ill to take part in any such hearing or give instructions to anyone else to take part on their behalf.

In the absence of such a policy and if the employee remains off on "stress" there are four options for keeping things moving:

a) Hold the meeting away from the workplace e.g. at the employee's home, with her agreement

b) Conduct the meeting by telephone

c) Conduct the discussion in writing

d) Allow the employee to send a representative (this is only really appropriate in a disciplinary scenario, rather than the performance issues that are being addressed here)

Of course it is best to incorporate the above points into the sickness and absence policy as well.

Question

In dealing with a long-term sick employee, the employee's own specialist disagrees with the report given by our occupational health adviser. Can we rely on our own medical evidence?

Solution

It has long been the case that an employer can rely on its own occupational health report over any information provided by the individual's GP. This is because the GP is primarily responsible for the care of the person, and does not necessarily have the occupational health perspective.

The same will apply where the occupational health report is being compared to a specialist report. Again, the specialist is likely to be focusing more on the individual and the condition, whereas the occupational health specialist is trained and qualified in assessing employees' fitness to work.

However, you should ensure that your occupational health adviser has had sight of the GP's report and a specialist's report when giving his/her advice. You can rely on the occupational health adviser's knowledge of your work environment and the work which the employee is required to do but the medical opinion of a specialist about the employee's diagnosis and prognosis is likely to be preferred over that of an occupational health adviser.

Question

An employee with a heavy manual job has been off sick for a long time, but the employer is convinced that he is capable of light work. Can the employer insist on this?

Solution

In the absence of a written light working policy as part of the sickness and absence procedures, it is difficult for an employer to insist that an employee should come back and perform light duties. It is therefore highly recommended that a light duties policy is built into those procedures.

In the absence of that feature of the policy, it is possible for the employer to achieve the same result by dismissing the employee from the existing job and making an offer of re-engagement in the light duties position. As the employer would be dismissing, the normal tests for dismissal apply, and there would have to be both a fair reason for dismissal and the dismissal for that reason has to be fair and reasonable in all circumstances. Therefore the employer would have to go through a full capability dismissal process prior to effecting the dismissal, and ensure compliance with the ACAS code.

If the employee failed to accept the offer of re-engagement in the light duties position then, whatever the merits of this dismissal claim, compensation is likely to be reduced by virtue of his refusal to mitigate loss by accepting an alternative position. Indeed, if the light duties job carries the same salary, there would arguably be a total failure to mitigate loss.

By explaining the above outcome to the employee, the employer may be able to persuade him to accept the light duties position.

Question

David, who has been off work for six months, has exhausted his right to receive contractual sickpay. You have written to him telling him this but he has written back saying: "I believe it would be reasonable for you to adjust your sick-pay scheme so that I continue to be paid".

What do you do?

Solution

David has no right to continue to be paid full pay once his contractual sick pay has been exhausted. Even if David has a disability it is not a reasonable adjustment to adjust the company sick pay scheme for disabled employees and continue to pay such employees after their entitlement to contractual sick pay had been exhausted.

This follows the case of O'Hanlon v Commissioners for HM Revenue & Customs. In this case it was held that when Mrs O'Hanlon's sick pay had been exhausted under HM Revenue and Customs' sick pay policy, the employer's failure to continue to pay Mrs O'Hanlon did not constitute a failure to make a reasonable adjustment.

In deciding this case reference was made to the fact that the reason for making reasonable adjustments is to enable employees to be able to 'play a full part in the world of work' and not 'treat them as objects of charity'.

Question

Neville, the office handyman/driver, suffered an accident which left him with badly damaged feet. You accept that this is a disability, which is a protected characteristic under the Equality Act. As a result of the accident Neville can no longer do his job. You have no other suitable vacancies at present.

What, if anything, can you do?

Solution

In analysing any potential disability discrimination case, the first step is to analyse whether or not the person is disabled. In this particular case it is agreed that the injury is severe enough to be classified as a disability.

The employer's duty to make reasonable adjustments is triggered. In the circumstances it is difficult to see how a handyman/driver with badly damaged feet could have his job adjusted so that he can continue to do it. Nonetheless the employer must go to considerable lengths to consider various options including where someone else could do the driving, or physical adjustments to the job which would enable Neville to continue to perform that role.

On the assumption that there are no reasonable adjustments, and there are no suitable vacancies, the question arises as to whether or not Neville can be dismissed. First, applying unfair dismissal law, Neville can be fairly dismissed on the grounds of capability, subject to following a correct procedure. Where an employee is rendered by reason of injury incapable of performing work, and there is no alternative vacancy, a fair dismissal can be effected.

Dismissal is a form of discrimination. Unlike various other categories of discrimination, however, direct disability discrimination, which this would be, can be justified. Here the justification is Neville cannot perform his job role and there are no suitable vacancies.

Provided therefore the employer goes through the correct process, it is possible to dismiss Neville fairly, and to avoid a successful disability discrimination claim.

Question

Can I withdraw discretionary profit share and bonus from employees on long term sickness?

Solution

Assuming that the contract of employment states that bonus and profit share payments are discretionary, they are likely to fall into one of the two following categories:

(a) Bonus/profit share payments that relate to work the employee has done – retroactive pay for work performed. In this case the bonus payments must be paid even to employees on sick leave but the payments can be pro-rated so that the employee only receives a bonus for the period that he or she was actually at work and working (i.e. prior to when he or she went on sick leave).

(b) Bonus/profit share payments paid to people in active employment to encourage future loyalty. In this case, if the employee is at work on the date that the bonus is paid, he or she should receive the full bonus. If he or she is absent due to sick leave on the date the bonus is paid, he or she would receive no bonus.

If the employee has a disability covered by the Equality Act the employee may well try to assert that a reasonable adjustment could be to continue to pay his or her bonus or profit share. However, an employee is unlikely to be able to persuade a tribunal that this is a reasonable adjustment. This is as a result of the case of O'Hanlon v Commissioners for HM Revenue & Customs (2008) in which an employee attempted to argue that by way of a reasonable adjustment her employers should have continued to pay her after she had exhausted her sick pay entitlement. The Employment Appeal Tribunal dismissed the claim on the basis that the provisions of the Disability Discrimination Act (now replaced by the Equality Act) are designed to require modifications that will enable them to play a full part in the world of work, not to produce a result that can act as a disincentive to return to work. By analogy this case is likely to extend to the payment of bonuses, so there is no need to make an adjustment.

Question

An airline recruitment manager has been told by his superior, when recruiting cabin crew, that he should "only recruit the pretty and handsome ones". Is this likely to lead to any problems?

Solution

On the face of it discriminating against a job applicant on the basis of their looks and whether the recruiter deems them to be pretty or handsome enough for the job is not going to fall foul of discrimination legislation. This is because discrimination claims can only be brought on the basis of one of the 9 'protected characteristics' covered by the Equality Act of sex, race, religion, disability, pregnancy and maternity, marriage and civil partnership, gender reassignment, age and sexual orientation. There is no such claim of discrimination because of prettiness or handsomeness (or lack thereof).

However, where a look-ism policy or job specification may breach discrimination law is where a job applicant does not get the job because of a disability, such as disfigurement, which renders him or her not pretty enough for the job. The job applicant in this instance may be able to bring a discrimination claim on the basis of the protected characteristic of 'disability'.

This recently happened in a tribunal case against the trendy outfitter, Abercrombie and Fitch. Abercrombie and Fitch enforced a 'look' policy which was contained within the staff handbook and detailed how employees should present themselves at work. Miss Dean breached the 'look' policy when she wore a cardigan to cover her prosthetic arm and was subsequently sent off the shop floor and told to work in the stock room for breaching the 'look' policy. Miss Dean won her case and received an award of £7800 in respect of injury to feelings.

In addition, if a look-ism policy indirectly discriminates on the basis of any protected characteristic a job applicant (if the policy is applied at the recruitment stage) or employee (if it is applied during the employee's employment) could then have grounds upon which he or she could bring a claim.

Question

Andrew went off sick a month ago; you have just got a medical report back from your occupational health doctor saying Andrew is suffering from alcohol-related depression and that he's unlikely to be fit to return to work for at least six months, after which he will need at least half a day off each week for treatment for at least a year. Could Andrew's condition be a disability under the Equality Act and, if so, what effect might this have on your decisions?

Solution

Andrew's manager might well take the view that he does not want to wait six months to see whether Andrew is well enough to return and also that he does not want to give Andrew half a day off every week for treatment; on that basis, Andrew's manager's preferred route might well be dismissal.

There are two possible claims Andrew could bring if his employment is terminated. The first is unfair dismissal.

The fair reason the company will have to rely on is "capability". We have a medical report which suggests that Andrew is unlikely to be fit to return to work for six months and that he will then need time off work for treatment. In order to conduct a fair dismissal, the company will need to invite Andrew to a meeting to discuss the medical report. You should then consider your decision. Considerations should include:

- The length of the absence
- Andrew's past service
- The importance of Andrew's job and the feasibility of employing a temporary replacement
- The effect of Andrew's absence on other employees
- Alternative employment

Provided any decision is within a band of reasonable responses, the tribunal should not interfere. However, it is worth remembering that an absence of six months is not all that unusual – for example it is the minimum amount of time that a woman on maternity leave would be likely to take.

The second potential claim is disability discrimination.

Addiction to alcohol, nicotine or any other substance will not of itself amount to an impairment under the Equality Act 2010. However, the Act does not look at how impairments are caused. Therefore, Andrew's depression could (subject to the usual tests) qualify as a disability even though it was caused by his alcoholism. Indeed, in the case of Power v Panasonic (2003), the Employment Appeal Tribunal held that depression caused by alcoholism was capable of being a disability.

Dismissing Andrew because of a lengthy period of absence followed by a requirement for regular days off could give rise to a claim of discrimination arising from disability (Section 15 Equality Act 2010). It will fall to the employer to show that the treatment was a proportionate means of achieving a legitimate aim.

The same factors that come into play under unfair dismissal (the importance of Andrew's job and feasibility of employing temporary cover) will also be relevant here. The employer will have to show a real business need for permanent cover from Andrew's job and that the same aim could not be met by less discriminating means. These sorts of cases always turn on their own facts but in general terms it is difficult to see how the employer here could argue that dismissal was a proportionate means of achieving a legitimate aim. Most employers can hold most jobs open for six months. Indeed, a tribunal might well view this as a reasonable adjustment – which the employer would be required to make under Section 20 Equality Act 2010.

MISCELLANEOUS

Question

Sam began working for his employer on 5 March 2010. His employment was terminated on 4 March 2011.

Does Sam have the requisite 12 months' 'continuous employment' to bring a claim in a tribunal against his employer for unfair dismissal?

Solution

Many would answer "no" because he did not work until 5 March 2011. However, for the purposes of submitting a claim in a tribunal for unfair dismissal Sam does have 12 months' 'continuous employment'. He therefore would be able to bring a claim for unfair dismissal. The day on which the employee started work is to be included in the computation of time.

This point was decided in Pacitti Jones v. O'Brien. Ms O'Brien commenced employment on 8 April 2002. On 27 March 2003, her employer delivered a letter to her home terminating her employment with one week's notice from that date. She was away and did not receive the letter until 31 March. Initially the tribunal found that the period of notice commenced on 28 March and expired on 3 April and that, accordingly, she had not been continuously employed for one year and thus could not claim unfair dismissal. On appeal, the Employment Appeal Tribunal (EAT) held that the period of notice commenced on 1 April and expired 7 April and that the claim for unfair dismissal was therefore admissible.

If the period of one year beginning with 8 April in one year did not end until 8 April in the succeeding year, a year would comprise 366 days (or 367, in a leap year), rather than 365.

Question

Carly is a receptionist at an accountant's firm. She lives within close walking distance of the office. Overnight there is a severe snow storm causing travel disruption and the authorities are advising people not to travel unless absolutely essential. Carly is able to walk to work but is unwilling to as she is accident prone and is scared of slipping on the icy pavements

Can you request that Carly attends work and take disciplinary action if she fails to do so?

Solution

The first issue is whether you can require Carly to attend work. There is a potential health and safety issue here. If authorities are telling people to stay at home unless their journey is essential, then you may not want to put too much pressure on people to return to work as employers have a duty of care to their employees and a potential liability may exist if employees were pressurised into travelling by car or foot when conditions were dangerous.

Employers need to take a balanced approach, and encourage employees to make reasonable efforts to attend work without putting pressure on them to travel. Employers should also remember that care should be taken not to breach the duty of mutual trust and confidence otherwise an employee may have grounds to resign and bring a constructive unfair dismissal claim.

However, if Carly does not come into work due to the adverse weather conditions, you do not have to pay her. Although, of course, you could exercise discretion and some alternative options available are to:

- Pay Carly for some or all of the absence
- Agree that Carly can use any accrued holiday to cover the absence
- Agree that Carly can set the time off against future overtime.

If in this example, you decide not to pay employees unable to attend work due to the adverse weather conditions or require employees to use their holiday to cover the absence, circulating this message to Carly and other employees may encourage employees to find ways to attend work.

With regard to the issue of whether disciplinary action can be taken against Carly, whilst an employer may contemplate taking disciplinary action, especially if there is a clause in the employee's contract which makes it clear that employees must make all reasonable effort to attend work, in this case it is likely to be difficult to demonstrate that Carly did not make all reasonable efforts and consequently it is likely to be difficult to justify taking disciplinary action.

Add these facts;

Carly is willing and able to walk to work but due to the ice her daughter's school is closed.

Carly is unable to make alternative childcare arrangements with such short notice and phones work to tell you that she cannot attend work. How do you treat Carly's leave?

Employees have the right to take a reasonable amount of unpaid leave to take necessary action to deal with situations affecting their dependants. It is certainly arguable that due to the unexpected closure of her daughter's school and the need for Carly to make last minute child care arrangements Carly will be able to rely on this right to take leave from work. Therefore in these circumstances you would treat Carly's time off as leave for the purpose of dealing with an emergency affecting a dependent.

Under the statutory scheme there is no right to paid time off in such circumstances and consequently the leave can be treated as unpaid.

Question

Gritbusters is a gritting company. Due to the "big freeze" their services have been heavily in demand, but three days into the crisis they have run out of grit. They have no work for their employees to do and consequently do not want to pay them.

Do they have to pay them?

Solution

Whilst Gritbusters have no available work to give to their employees, staff are still entitled to be paid, unless there is an express clause giving Gritbusters the right to lay employees off for a short period. A clause simply stating *'we reserve the right to lay you off without pay or to put you on short time working'* will suffice. We recommend employers to have this clause in contracts of employment.

If Gritbusters do not have the express right to lay employees off, another option available to Gritbusters is to require employees to use their holiday to cover the absence. Under the Working Time Regulations employers must give notice of double the length of the holiday, so if Gritbusters want the employees to take one day's leave they will need to serve employees with two days' notice.

Consequently, this is unlikely to assist Gritbusters, especially if it is the case that Gritbusters only needs employees to stay off work for one or two days.

Other alternative options rely on the employees' goodwill such as the employees agreeing to use their holiday to cover the absence, or the employees agreeing to set the time off against future overtime.

If employees do agree to these alternative measures then it is advisable to confirm this in writing so that you can refer to this in the event of a later dispute.

Question

Rory joined us recently. We sent a reference request to his previous employer which came back with the following wording:

"At the time of termination, Rory was under investigation for theft, but left before our enquiries were completed".

In the circumstances we have decided not to confirm Rory's appointment and have terminated his employment. Rory then produced some evidence to us which clearly demonstrated that the allegation of theft against him could not be sustained, and that he would not have been dismissed. If we refuse to continue his employment, does Rory have any come back against us?

Solution

Probably not. An employer has a wide discretion as to whether or not to recruit an employee and when an offer is made "subject to satisfactory references" the employer has a wide discretion as to what that phrase means. Rory has of course only been there a short time and therefore will not qualify for unfair dismissal.

The former employer is however in a much more difficult position. Where a reference has been given that is inaccurate or misleading, the giver of the reference can be sued in negligence. In the case of Cox v Sun Alliance, Sun Alliance indicated that there were unresolved disciplinary matters. Although this was technically accurate, it was held to be misleading. The Court of Appeal found that the former employer was negligent in providing a reference to subsequent employers which relied upon allegations of dishonest conduct which they had not properly investigated. The damages awarded against a former employer in this case can be significant, in that it will be based on the employee's loss of earnings from the new post. Consequently, any employer giving a reference should be cautious and either decline to give a reference, or limit any reference to purely factual information such as dates of employment and job title in order to limit the risk of a claim from a former employee.

Question

Tim is a new recruit in a team of engineers. Roger, the manager, suspects that his workers are taking unauthorised smoke breaks. Roger feels that he can trust Tim, and asks him to keep a log of who is smoking and when. Tim says that it is against the law to "spy" on fellow employees and refuses. Roger finds a reason for Tim failing his probation.

Where does the employer stand?

Is your answer different if instead of being terminated, Tim is moved to an unpopular and difficult project, a longer distance from his home?

Solution

Although most claims of unfair dismissal require a 12 month qualifying period, where a whistleblowing claim is brought under the Public Interest Disclosure Act 1998, there is no qualifying period of service and, if the employee is successful, the dismissal is automatically unfair. So although Tim has short service, he can bring an unfair dismissal claim.

Although sneaky, and one can understand Tim's reluctance, it is not against the law to "spy" in this way. Tim is therefore incorrect in his assertion that Roger's request is illegal. Does this therefore mean that his claim for a whistleblowing based unfair dismissal will fail? The case of Babula v Waltham Forest (2007) established that an employee disclosure can qualify as whistleblowing even if no legal obligation actually exists, provided the employee had good reasons to believe that there is a breach of a legal obligation, and acted in good faith. In this case if Tim can demonstrate that he genuinely believed that spying was against the law then his claim is likely to succeed, even though he was mistaken.

If, instead of being terminated, Tim is kept on but receives detrimental treatment such as being given unattractive work, lack of training, lack of promotion etc it is still possible for him to bring a claim. Under Section 47B of Employment Rights Act, detrimental treatment arising as a result of whistleblowing, where there is no dismissal, can result in a valid claim for compensation. There is no financial cap on the compensation, which is assessed on a similar basis as a discrimination claim.

Question

We have received an anonymous letter alleging that there has been dishonest practice within the company. How do we handle this?

Solution

There is no strictly correct way of handling this. It very much comes down to an employer's judgement. Ways of dealing with this are:

(a)   Completely ignoring the letter.

(b)   Investigating the alleged dishonest practice with the persons named in the letter. Perhaps it is possible to investigate some of the allegations without alerting the members of staff, and if so, it may be possible to establish whether there is any truth in the allegations.

(c)   Sending a communication to every employee in the company stating that an anonymous letter has been received and that the company is unable to act on such correspondence, but that if the employee concerned wishes to come forward the company will guarantee anonymity and protection.

It is possible to have a policy on anonymous letters within the handbook, stating that such letters will not be acted upon and that if anyone has any concerns they should come forward using a prescribed process under which the person will be protected. Hopefully this will be a deterrent against anonymous letter writing.

Financial malpractice is capable of being a whistleblowing claim. Therefore if at some stage you do identify the author of the anonymous letter, that person must not be treated detrimentally as a result of the anonymous letter. Although it is unlikely that the whistleblowing legislation will apply to a situation whereby information has been given anonymously, as soon as that person has been identified, he or she could provide the information through another process which would qualify for protection.

In running a disciplinary, it is possible, in a reasonably extreme case, to use anonymous witness statements (see page 73).

Question

Frank Acorn was employed by Treetowers plc as Sales Director for 3 years. After resigning, he wrote to Treetowers plc to make a data subject access request pursuant to section 7 of the Data Protection Act 1998.

In his request, Frank asked for their search to be confined to data concerning specific events and happenings, which he listed in his letter. He also requested that search tools be used to identify some of his personal data, which he said would most likely be held in the form of sent and received emails and word-processed documents.

In addition to this, Frank asked for a copy of his personnel file and suggested that when searching email records, they also search under variants of his name – i.e Frank, FA etc

Once Treetowers plc have identified all of the personal data within the scope of his request, Frank asked that Treetowers plc provide him with a copy of the information constituting personal data and also:

Provide a description of the data

Explain the purposes for which the data is processed

Identify the source or sources of the data

Set out to whom the data has been disclosed or may be disclosed

With his letter, Frank enclosed a cheque for £10 in respect of the maximum prescribed fee and said he looked forward to hearing from Treetowers plc within the statutory time limit of 40 days.

Your IT manger says that it will take 100 hours to run a search, and that he believes there will be over 10,000 emails and 500 documents to be considered.

How would you go about Frank's request? Are Treetowers plc legally obliged to comply with his requests?

Solution

Although onerous and time consuming, you are legally obliged to comply with the majority of Frank's requests.

The Data Protection Act was originally enacted in 1984 and has always covered computer records. Quite simply, information held on a computer that is "personal data" about Frank is disclosable. This will include personal data held on:

- Databases
- Word Processing Systems
- Emails
- Automated payroll systems
- Records of automated door entry systems such as swipe cards

You can see from the above that the potential is very wide indeed. Frank has limited his request to "emails and word processed documents", which clearly do fall within the scope of what is covered by the Data Protection Act.

As to the sequence of events in responding to Frank's request, there are various exclusions and exemptions.

The correct process is first to collate all data that could possibly be covered by the Act, and then assess whether or not any of the exemptions do apply.

As to the practicalities of recovering this information held on computer, it is onerous, but nonetheless feasible. Frank is correct in stating that this data can be identified through the use of search tools and is also correct that in undertaking the searches you should also search under the abbreviations of his name.

With respect to providing Frank with a copy of the information, you must comply with this. He is ultimately entitled to a copy of the information, but note that this does not have to be a hard copy. For example, emails and word-processed documents could be burned onto a CD, which may make the process slightly easier. He is also entitled to the other information set out in his four bullet points about the description, purpose, source and disclosure of the data.

As mentioned earlier, there are various qualifications, exemptions and exceptions that may apply. The most important of these are:

Data must be "personal data". "Personal" has been defined as "biographical in a significant sense", and must have the individual as its focus. Thus, emails simply stating that Frank would be at a meeting, or copying him into an email about something, or seeking his opinion about some aspect of the business, would not be "about" Frank and therefore would not be personal data.

Care is needed, if complying with the request might result in the disclosure of information relating to another individual. The overriding rule is that the employer should supply as much information as can be supplied without disclosing the identity of the third party. The employer may seek the consent of the third party to disclose the information, and if the third party consents, the employer must disclose the information. There is however no obligation to seek consent.

Personal data processed in connection with management forecasting or planning, to the extent that complying with the request would be prejudice to the conduct of the business, is exempt from disclosure. For example, if information on a forthcoming sale or acquisition, or on a staff redundancy process would be disclosed through this request before the information is made public, it is likely to prejudice the conduct of a business.

Personal data consisting of records of intentions relating to negotiations between the employer and the employee, to the extent that the request would be likely to prejudice the negotiations is also exempt from disclosure. This would apply if, for example, there was a Compromise Agreement in the offing and emails were being exchanged about the level of offer.

There are specific provisions with the Act for dealing with onerous requests. It is possible for a company to ask the Information Commissioner to intervene, but his guidance clearly states that it is only in a very extreme case that he is likely to intervene.

Correspondence with lawyers is excluded under the professional privilege rule.

All the above relates to computer records and, although these kinds of requests have only recently become commonplace, the law is essentially unchanged since 1984. More recently, the Data Protection Act was extended to include documents as well as computer records. In dealing with requests for paper records, the principle of personal data also applies. There is another limitation that only arises when considering paper records. That is that the documents must be kept in a relevant filing system. The courts have defined this as a system that is of "sufficient sophistication to provide the same or similar ready accessibility as a computerised filing system". Thus, a relevant filing system is limited to a system in which the files are structured or referenced in such a way as to clearly indicate whether specific information capable of amounting to personal data is held within the system. Commentators have been debating over the last few years whether or not personnel files are sufficiently organised and accessible to come within this definition. This can often come down to consideration of very finely detailed points, such as whether someone unfamiliar with the file could open it, and within a couple of minutes quickly find sick certificates relating to a particular period. Is the file sub divided into different sections, including sick certificates, and is it filed in date order? The pragmatic view taken by most employers is that personnel files are covered by these definitions and are therefore disclosable.

No document that is embarrassing or prejudicial to the author or Treetowers plc can be excluded. If the company fails to disclose a document, then Frank has various remedies. He can apply to the Information Commissioner asking the Commissioner to determine whether or not his request has been carried out lawfully. In a more extreme case he can also apply to the court alleging a breach of the Data Protection rules which, if he can prove that he has suffered damage, may result in a claim for compensation. An employer has a defence to a claim for damages if it can prove that it had taken such steps as were reasonable in the circumstances to comply with the Data Protection rules. See also page 64.

Question

An employee is dismissed with a termination date of 30th September.

What is the last day on which this employee can bring a tribunal claim for sex discrimination?

Is the answer different if the employee raises a grievance?

Solution

A discrimination claim must be submitted three months from the date the act complained of was done or, where there is a continuing act of discrimination, three months from the date of the last act of discrimination.

In this case, assuming that the dismissal is being relied on as the act of discrimination or last act where there has been a continuing act of discrimination, the last day on which the employee can bring a sex discrimination claim is the 29th December. Note that it is not the 30th December, as this would be three months and a day. In one case an employee's claim was not accepted when it was e-mailed to the tribunal 88 seconds too late. The deadline is applied strictly.

The tribunal does have jurisdiction to extend the time limit for bringing a sex discrimination claim if it feels that it would be 'just and equitable' to do so taking into account all the circumstances. However, an employee has to have a convincing story to be able to satisfy a tribunal that the deadline should be extended, for example illness or other incapacity.

The answer is not different if the employee raises a grievance. Under the old statutory dispute resolution procedures, there were provisions for an automatic three-month extension of time in certain circumstances to allow extra time for grievance procedures or disciplinary appeals to continue. In particular, in cases where a Claimant raised a grievance alleging discrimination, the time limit for bringing a discrimination claim could be extended by a further three months. The SDRPs were abolished, however, on 6 April 2009 and there is no automatic extension of time under the new regime even if an appeal is still ongoing or a grievance has been raised.

Question

We have recruited a new manager, who is paid more than similar managers. They have complained that under Equal Pay, they should all be paid the same. Is this correct?

Solution

No. The Equal Pay Act addresses the disparity in pay between males and females. Thus, for example, a female group of canteen staff could complain that a male group of gardeners perform work rated as equivalent or of equal value but have higher pay. Furthermore, if the employer can show a genuine material factor (that is not itself tainted by sex discrimination) why the pay-rates are different then it will be able to rebut the presumption of discrimination.

Here, although we do not know the gender of the managers, it is likely that there is a mixed group of males and females, meaning that the Equal Pay Act has no application. In addition, it is unlikely that the new manager is paid the salary that he/she is receiving as a result of his/her gender.

On a broader note, there is no legal requirement to treat employees equally, reasonably or fairly. In a severe case, failure to do so could result in a constructive dismissal, but there is no general law as such that the employer has to behave in a reasonable or fair manner.